MW01680307

HAMAS AND ISRAEL: CONFLICTING STRATEGIES OF GROUP-BASED POLITICS

Sherifa Zuhur

December 2008

*****

*****

Comments pertaining to this report are invited and should be forwarded to: Director, Strategic Studies Institute, U.S. Army War College, 122 Forbes Ave, Carlisle, PA 17013-5244.

*****

All Strategic Studies Institute (SSI) publications are available on the SSI homepage for electronic dissemination. Hard copies of this report also may be ordered from our homepage. SSI's homepage address is: *www.StrategicStudiesInstitute.army.mil.*

*****

The Strategic Studies Institute publishes a monthly e-mail newsletter to update the national security community on the research of our analysts, recent and forthcoming publications, and upcoming conferences sponsored by the Institute. Each newsletter also provides a strategic commentary by one of our research analysts. If you are interested in receiving this newsletter, please subscribe on our homepage at *www.StrategicStudiesInstitute.army.mil/newsletter/.*

ISBN 1-58487-371-X

CONTENTS

FOREWORD

This monograph considers the changing fortunes of the Palestinian movement, HAMAS, and the recent outcomes of Israeli strategies aimed against this group and Palestinian nationalism external to the Fatah faction of the Palestinian Authority. The example of HAMAS challenges much of the current wisdom on "insurgencies" and their containment. As the author, Dr. Sherifa Zuhur, demonstrates, efforts have been made to separate HAMAS from its popular support and network of social and charitable organizations. These have not been effective in destroying the organization, nor in eradicating the will to resist among a fairly large segment of the Palestinian population.

It is important to consider this Islamist movement in the context of a region-wide phenomenon of similar movements with local goals, which can be persuaded to relinquish violence, or which could move in the opposite direction, becoming more violent. Certainly an orientation to HAMAS and its base must be factored into new and more practical and effective approaches to peacemaking.

At the same time, HAMAS offers a fascinating instance of the dynamics of strategic reactions, and the modification of Israeli impulses towards aggressive deterrence, as well as evolution in the Islamist movements' planning and operations. As well, the Palestinian-Israeli conflict bears similarities to a long-standing civil conflict, even as it has sparked inter-Palestinian hostilities in its most recent phase.

The need for informed and critical discussion of the future of Islamism in the region continues today. We offer this monograph to those who wish to consider this particular aspect of the Palestinian-Israeli-Arab conflict.

DOUGLAS C. LOVELACE, JR.
Director
Strategic Studies Institute

BIOGRAPHICAL SKETCH OF THE AUTHOR

SHERIFA ZUHUR is Research Professor of Islamic and Regional Studies at the Strategic Studies Institute. She has many years of field experience in the region and specialized in the study of Islamist movements since the late 1970s. She has lectured internationally, and held faculty positions in American and Middle Eastern universities including MIT, the University of California, Berkeley, the American University in Cairo, and the Chaim Herzog Center for Middle Eastern Studies and Diplomacy at Ben Gurion University of the Negev. Dr. Zuhur is also currently the Director of the Institute for Middle Eastern, Islamic, and Diasporic Studies and an Associate Editor of the Bulletin of the Middle Eastern Studies Association. She has published 16 books or monographs, and more than 116 articles or chapters in edited books and is a contributing editor of the *Encyclopedia of Arab-Israeli Wars* (2008) and the *Encyclopedia of (US) Middle Eastern Wars*. Among her studies are *Precision in the Global War on Terror: Inciting Muslims through the War of Ideas* (2008); *Iran, Iraq and the United States: The New Triangle's Impact on Sectarianism and the Nuclear Threat* (2006); *One Hundred Osamas: Islamist Threats and the Future of Counterinsurgency* (2005), and *Egypt: Security, Political, and Islamist Challenges* (2007). She has most recently written a monograph on the counterterrorism program in Saudi Arabia. Dr. Zuhur holds a B.A. in Political Science and Arabic, a Masters in Islamic Studies, and a Ph.D. in Middle Eastern History, all from the University of California, Los Angeles.

SUMMARY

The conflict between Palestinians and Israelis has heightened since 2001, even as any perceived threat to Israel from Egypt, Jordan, Iraq, or even Syria, has declined. Israel, according to Chaim Herzog, Israel's sixth President, had been "born in battle" and would be "obliged to live by the sword."[1] Yet, the Israeli government's conquest and occupation of the West Bank and Gaza brought about a very difficult challenge, although resistance on a mass basis was only taken up years later in the First Intifadha. Israel could not tolerate Palestinian Arabs' resistance of their authority on the legal basis of denial of self-determination,[2] and eventually preferred to grant some measures of self-determination while continuing to consolidate control of the Occupied Territories, the West Bank, East Jerusalem, and Gaza. However, a comprehensive peace, shimmering in the distance, has eluded all. Inter-Israeli and inter-Palestinian divisions deepened as peace danced closer before retreating.

Israel's stance towards the democratically-elected Palestinian government headed by HAMAS in 2006, and towards Palestinian national coherence—legal, territorial, political, and economic—has been a major obstacle to substantive peacemaking. The reasons for recalcitrant Israeli and HAMAS stances illustrate both continuities and changes in the dynamics of conflict since the Oslo period (roughly 1994 to the al-Aqsa Intifadha of 2000). Now, more than ever, a long-term truce and negotiations are necessary. These could lead in stages to that mirage-like peace, and a new type of security regime.

The rise in popularity and strength of the HAMAS (Harakat al-Muqawama al-Islamiyya, or Movement of the Islamic Resistance) Organization and its interaction with Israel is important to an understanding of Israel's "Arab" policies and its approach to counterterrorism and counterinsurgency. The crisis brought about by the electoral success of HAMAS in 2006 also challenged Western powers' commitment to democratic change in the Middle East because Palestinians had supported the organization in the polls. Thus, the viability of a two-state solution rested on an Israeli acknowledgement of the Islamist movement, HAMAS, and on Fatah's ceding power to it.

Shifts in Israel's stated national security objectives (and dissent over them) reveal HAMAS' placement at the nexus of Israel's domestic, Israeli-Palestinian, and regional objectives. Israel has treated certain enemies differently than others: Iran, Hizbullah, and Islamist Palestinians (whether HAMAS, supporters of Islamic Jihad, or the Islamic Movement inside Israel) all fall into a particular rubric in which Islamism—the most salient and enduring socio-religious movement in the Middle East in the wake of Arab nationalism—is identified with terrorism and insurgency rather than with group politics and identity. The antipathy to religious fervor was somewhat ironic in light of Israel's own expanding "religious" (*haredim*) groups. In Israel's earlier decades, Islamic identity politics were understood and successfully repressed, as Israelis did not want to allow any repetition of the Palestinian Mufti's nationalism or the Qassamiyya (the armed brigades in the 1936-39 rebellion).

Yet at the same time, identity politics and religious attitudes were not eradicated, but were inside of Israel, bringing about great inequality as well as physical and psychological separation of the Jewish and non-Jewish populations.[3] This represented efforts to control politically and physically the now 20 percent Arab minority, and dealt with the demographic threat constantly spoken of in Israel by warding off intermarriage, limiting property control and rights, and physical access. Still today, some Israeli politicians call for an exodus by Palestinian-Israelis (so-called Arab-Israelis) in some areas, who they wish to resettle in the West Bank.

For decades, Muslim religious properties and institutions were managed under Jewish supervision—substantial inter-Israeli conflict over that supervision notwithstanding[4]—and this allowed for a continuing stereotype of the recalcitrant, anti-modern Muslims and Arabs who were punished for any expression of Palestinian (or Arab) nationalism by replacing them—imams or qadis, for instance—with more quiescent Israeli Muslims, and by retaining Jewish control over endowment (*waqf*), properties, and income.

Contemporary Islamism took hold in Palestinian society, as it has throughout the Middle East and has, to a great degree, supplanted secular nationalism. This is problematic in terms of the conflict between Israel and the Palestinians because the official Israeli position towards key Islamists—Iran, Hizbullah, and the Palestinian groups like HAMAS, Islamic Jihad, or Hizb al-Tahrir—characterizes them as Israel-haters and terrorists. They have become the existential threat to Israel (along with Iran) since the demise of Saddam Hussein in Iraq.

Israel steadfastly rejected diplomacy and truce offers by HAMAS for 8 months in 2008, despite an earlier truce that held for several years. By the spring of 2008, continued rejection of a truce was politically risky as Prime Minister Ehud Olmert teetered on the edge of indictment by his own party and finally had to announce his resignation in the summer. In fact, on his way out the door, Olmert announced a peace plan that ignores HAMAS and many demands of the Palestinian Authority as a whole ever since Oslo. If the plan was merely to create a sense of Olmert's legacy, it is not altogether clear why it offered so little compromise.

On the other hand, Israelis have for over a year[5] been discussing the wisdom of reconquering the Gaza Strip (a prospect that would aid the Fatah side of the Palestinian Authority) and also engage in "preemptive deterrence" or attacks on other states in the region. This could happen at any time if the truce between Israel and HAMAS breaks down, although the risks of any of these enterprises would be high. A potential deal with Syria was also announced by Olmert, similarly, perhaps, to stave off his own resignation, and Syria made a counteroffer.[6] Turkish-mediated indirect talks were to continue at the time of this writing, though they might be rescheduled.[7] Support for an Israeli attack on Iran continues to play well in the Israeli media, despite the fact that Israelis argue fiercely about the wisdom of such a course. All of this shows flux in the region, with Israel in its customary strong, but concerned position.

HAMAS emerged as the chief rival to the secularist-nationalist framework of Fatah, the dominant member of the Palestine Liberation Organization (PLO). This occurred as Palestinians rebelled against the worsening conditions they experienced following the Oslo Peace Accords. HAMAS' political and strategic development has been both ignored and misreported in Israeli and Western sources which villainize the group, much as the PLO was once characterized as an anti-Semitic terrorist group.[8] Relatively few detailed treatments in English counter the media blitz that reduces HAMAS to its early, now defunct, 1988 charter.

Disagreements within the Israeli military and political establishments over the national security objectives of that country reveal HAMAS' placement at the nexus of Israel's domestic, Palestinian, and regional objectives. This process can be traced back to Ariel Sharon's formation of the KADIMA Party and decision to withdraw unilaterally from Gaza without engaging in a peace process with Palestinians. This reflected a new understanding that Arab armies were unlikely to launch any successful attack against Israel, but Israel should focus instead on protecting its Jewish citizens via barrier methods.[9]

This new thinking coexists alongside the long-standing policies described by Yitzhak Shamir as aggressive defense; in other words, offensives aimed at increasing Israel's strategic depth, or attacking potential threats in neighboring countries—as in the raid on the nearly completed nuclear power facility at Osirak, Iraq, in 1981, or the mysterious Operation ORCHARD carried out on a weapons cache in Syria in September 2007, or in the invasions, air, and ground wars (1978, 1982, 2006) in Lebanon.

Israelis considered occupied Palestinian territories valuable in land-for-peace negotiations. During the Oslo process, according to Israelis, Israel was ready to withdraw entirely to obtain peace.[10] Actually, the value of land to trade for peace and costs of maintaining security for the settlers there, as well as containing the uprisings, were complicated equations. Palestinians and others argue that, in fact, Israel offered no more in the various proposed exchanges than the less valuable portion of the western West Bank and Gaza, and refused to deal with outstanding issues such as the fate of Palestinian refugees (4,913,993 Palestinians live outside of Israel[11] and the occupied territories; 1,337,388 according to UNRWA[12]—registered refugees—live in camps, and 3,166,781 live outside of camps),[13] prisoners, water, and the claim of Jerusalem as a capital.

Many Arabs believe that Israel never intended the formation of a Palestinian state, and that its land-settlement policies during the Oslo period provide proof of its true intentions. Either way, the "Oslo optimism" faded away between Israelis and Palestinians with the al-Aqsa (Second) Intifadha in October 2000.

The Israeli Right, and part of its Left, claimed that the diplomatic collapse, plus Arafat's government's corruption, showed there was no "partner to peace." Another segment of the Israeli Left has continued until this day to argue for land-for-peace and complete withdrawal from the territories.

According to Barry Rubin, the Israeli military felt the Palestinian threat would not increase, and that if settlers could be evacuated and a stronger line of defense erected, they might better defend their citizenry. That defense could not be achieved with suicide attacks ongoing in Israeli population centers. When earlier Israeli strategies had not achieved an end to Palestinian Islamist violence, Israelis had pushed this task onto the Fatah-dominated Palestinian Authority in the 1990s.[14] Pointing to the failures of the Palestinian Authority, the new Israeli "securitist" (*bitchonist,* in Hebrew, or security-focused) strategy moved away from negotiations, and called for further separation and segregation of the Israeli population from Palestinians. Neither a full-blown physical resistance by Palestinians, including suicide attacks, or the missiles launched from Gaza could be dealt with in this manner. The first depended on granting Palestinians rights to partial self-government, and the missile attacks were negotiated in Israel's June 2008 truce.

Israel claimed significant victories in its war against Palestinians by the use of targeted killings of leadership, boycotts, power cuts, preemptive attacks and detentions, and punishments to militant's families, relatives, and neighborhoods etc., because its counterterrorism logic is to reduce insurgents' organizational capability. This particular type of Israeli analysis rejects the idea that counterterrorist violence can spark more resistance and violence,[15] but one proponent also admitted that Israel had not "defeated the will to resistance" [of Palestinians].[16] This admission suggests that the tactics employed might not be indefinitely manageable, and that Palestinians, despite every possible effort made to weaken or incriminate them, to discourage or prevent their Arab non-Palestinian supporters from defending their interests, and to buy the services of collaborators, could edge Israelis back toward comprehensive negotiations, or rise up again against them. Moshe Sharett, Israel's second Prime Minister, once asked: "Do people consider that when military reactions outstrip in their severity the events that caused them, grave processes are set in motion which widen the gulf and thrust our neighbors into the extremist camp? How can this deterioration be halted?"[17]

HAMAS and its new wave of political thought, which had supported armed resistance along with the aim to create an Islamic society, had overtaken Fatah in popularity. Fatah, with substantial U.S. support edged closer to Israeli positions over 2006-07, promising to diminish Palestinian resistance, although President Mahmud Abbas had no means to do so, and could not even ensure Fatah's survival in the West Bank without HAMAS assent, and had been routed from Gaza.

Negotiating solely with the weaker Palestinian party—Fatah—cannot deliver the security Israel requires. This may lead Israel to reconquer the Gaza Strip or the West Bank and continue engaging in "preemptive deterrence" or attacks on other states in the region in the longer term.

The underlying strategies of Israel and HAMAS appear mutually exclusive and did not, prior to the summer of 2008, offer much hope of a solution to the Israeli-Palestinian-Arab conflict. Yet each side is still capable of revising its desired endstate and of necessary concessions to establish and preserve a long-term truce, or even a longer-term peace.

ENDNOTES - SUMMARY

1. Chaim Herzog, *The Arab-Israeli Wars: War and Peace in the Middle East: From the War of Independence through Lebanon*, New York: Random House, 1982, p. 362.

2. John Quigley, *Palestine and Israel: A Challenge to Justice*, Durham and London: Duke University Press, 1990, pp. 189-197.

3. Many works deal with this issue. A detailed study of the city of Acre is instructive. Rebecca L. Torstrick, *The Limits of Coexistence: Identity Politics in Israel*, Ann Arbor: University of Michigan Press, 2000.

4. Alisa Rubin Peled, *Debating Islam in the Jewish State: The Development of Policy Toward Islamic Institutions in Israel*, Albany: State University of New York Press, 2001.

5. Personal interviews, August 2008. Also see Pierre Razoux, "Mission Report to Israel, May 24-31, 2008," NATO Defense College.

6. *Associated Press*, September 4, 2008.

7. *Jerusalem Post*, September 8, 2008; also see Ramzy Baroud, "The Syria-Israel Peace Gambit," *Pacific Free Press*, September 14, 2008.

8. Ali Abunimeh, "Hamas and the Two-State Solution: Villain, Victim, or Missing Ingredient," *Middle East Policy*, Vol. XV, No. 3, Summer 2008, pp. 15-16.

9. Barry Rubin, "Israel's New Strategy," *Foreign Affairs*, Vol. 85, Issue 4, July/August 2006, pp. 111-112.

10. *Ibid*.

11. Source: PCBS, Mid-year 2004 Estimates, Statistical Abstract, No. 6, 2005.

12. United Nations Relief and Works Agency for Palestine Refugees in the Near East.

13. Source: UNRWA HQ, *UNRWA in Figures*, June 2007.

14. Glenn E. Robinson, *Building a Palestinian State: The Incomplete Revolution*, Bloomington: Indiana University Press, 1997, p. 189.

15. Hillel Frisch, "Motivation or Capabilities? Israeli Counterterrorism against Palestinian Suicide Bombings and Violence," *Mideast Security and Policy Studies*, Begin-Sadat Center for Strategic Studies, Bar Ilan University, December 2006. All, and countering Mia Bloom, pp. 1-3.

16. Statement by Israeli military personnel, June 2006.

17. As cited in Michael Brecher, *The Foreign Policy System of Israel, Setting, Images, Process*, New Haven: Yale University Press, 1972, p. 287.

HAMAS AND ISRAEL: CONLICTING STRATEGIES OF GROUP-BASED POLITICS

Introduction.

The conflict between Palestinians and Israelis has heightened since 2001, while at the same time any major military threat to Israel from Egypt, Jordan, Iraq, or even Syria, has visibly declined. Israel, according to Chaim Herzog, Israel's sixth President, had been "born in battle," and would be "obliged to live by the sword."[1] Yet, the Israeli government's conquest and occupation of the West Bank and Gaza brought about a very difficult challenge, although resistance on a mass basis was only taken up years later in the First Intifadha. Israel could not tolerate Palestinian Arabs' resistance of their authority on the legal basis of denial of self-determination,[2] and eventually preferred to grant some measures of self-determination while continuing to consolidate control of the territories. However, a comprehensive peace, shimmering in the distance, has eluded all. Inter-Israeli and inter-Palestinian divisions deepened as peace danced closer before retreating.

Israel's stance towards the democratically-elected Palestinian government headed by HAMAS in 2006 has been a major obstacle to substantive peacemaking. The reasons for Israel's position, and HAMAS' continuing verbal support of resistance, even as a fragile truce took hold on June 19, 2008, leads us to examine this relationship.

Since the outset of the Second, or Al-Aqsa, Intifadha in 2000,[3] Israeli security forces have killed 4,718 Palestinians and 10 foreign citizens. Palestinians have killed 236 Israeli civilians, 244 Israeli security forces, and 17 foreign citizens.[4] The numbers of dead and injured would be greatly inflated if we calculated the casualties in all of the Israeli-Arab wars. Another very negative outcome of the conflict that has inhibited Palestinian social and political development is the large numbers of Palestinians detained and imprisoned, more than 700,000 since 1967, and the vast majority were political prisoners. Today, some 8,500 (Israel's figure)[5] to 11,229 (the Mandela Institute's figure) are in prison, including 375 juveniles, 104 women, and some 870 to 836 (B'tselem's figure) are administrative detainees, in addition to about 3,000 at the time of this writing held by the Palestinian Authority (PA) (who primarily represent HAMAS prisoners of the Fatah-dominated PA in the West Bank). It is difficult to find a Palestinian man, certainly not a HAMAS member of a certain age who has not experienced several temporary detentions and incarcerations. Israel's High Court banned torture in 1999 but still practices isolation, prolonged interrogation, threats to family members, and denial of access to lawyers.

The conflict has moreover become a Muslim cause, and at the same time, remains a national one. To make matters worse, the Palestinian use of suicide attacks increased since their first appearance in the 1990s as a tactic to avenge Israeli killings of Palestinian civilians.[6] The many suicide attacks, often by self-recruited individuals, that became more frequent since 2000-01, presented a major challenge to Israel's defense of its population centers. The attractions of martyrdom were not a phenomenon that could easily be extinguished by the Palestinian leadership, particularly when it had nothing concrete to offer its population in its stead, and the condition of that population had worsened, not improved, in the Oslo era. As peace agreements between Israel and Egypt and Jordan had cancelled out the possibility of effective Arab resistance to Israel, only Palestinian bottom-up or popular action remained an option to Palestinians unable to obtain relief through diplomacy or political participation. Nevertheless, Palestinians, and even HAMAS, moved in these latter directions.

The 2006 electoral success, subsequent Western and Israeli boycott of the HAMAS organization, and factional strife among Palestinians are important to an understanding of Islamist movements, counterterrorism, counterinsurgency, and political development.

HAMAS' strategic development will be described more fully below. HAMAS members' internal debate on armed resistance is long-standing. As Dr. Naser El-Din Al-Shaer, former Dean of the Islamic University and Minister of Education until the HAMAS government was "fired" by Abbas, and a moderate who met with former President Jimmy Carter, explained:

> If there is any attack on the Israelis, they speak of terrorism and terrorism, and more terrorism. If Hamas and Islamic Jihad and all of these armed groups [such as Al Aqsa Martyrs Brigade] cease attacking Israel, then Israel will say: "Look, they've lost their power; and they can do nothing against us, so we are not going to give them anything."
>
> So by which means will Israel give our land back to us? If we are fully sovereign and we can attack the Israelis, then they identify us as we are terrorists and the whole world is supposed to side with them against us. And if we talk about peace, they said, "look they aren't able to do anything, so look let us give them nothing." So which language do they understand?[7]

Current Context.

HAMAS confronted the dismantling of its educational and social initiatives over all the West Bank one and a half years after it began its struggle to govern. Citizens of West Bank towns were mistreated, brutally beaten, and detained on a nightly basis, not only by the Israeli Defense Force (IDF) but also by Fatah-allied PA security officers.[8] In just 1 week, Israel made 38 military raids or incursions into the West Bank, killing a child, wounding two others, and abducting 48 civilians (without charge) including juveniles. This included a raid into al-Far`a refugee camp, responding to children demonstrating at the funeral of the child killed, and a demonstration against the separation Wall at Bil`in.[9] This was perhaps a typical week in the West Bank, which, according to the Western media, is being peacefully controlled by the PA. Al-Shaer commented on those tortured in PA custody, including a 67-year-old man who had suffered a cerebral hemorrhage from severe beating. PA officers raided and closed the Islamic schools and charities, including one with 1,000 students, in Nablus, Hebron, and Jenin—which have large concentrations of HAMAS supporters—and their institutional boards were reconstituted with Fatah members. This is regarded widely as the PA's efforts to follow Israeli (and perceived American) directions to root out HAMAS' social support structure. Some 2,000 persons were arrested.

Shaer complained that the Abbas-controlled West Bank displayed a policy of "violence, not security," and reported other scandalous types of corruption ongoing in the Fayyad-managed government headed by Abbas. He warned again that the population only sees a choice between continued humiliation and a mass popular resistance, and that it might be impossible to reason against a new Intifadha.[10] Just a day earlier, on August 10, Palestinians had responded to the campaign against HAMAS with a demonstration calling for national unity.[11]

HAMAS Roots in Short.

HAMAS was at first a social and educational initiative of certain actors, primarily Shaykh Ahmed Yasin (c. 1937-2004) from within the Palestinian branch of the Muslim Brotherhood movement. Yasin's natal village of al-Jura was destroyed during the 1948 war, and his family fled to Gaza. He became a quadriplegic after an accident at the age of 12, and attended al-Azhar University in Cairo, where he was attracted to the Muslim Brotherhood.

HAMAS inherited all the hallmarks of a Muslim Brotherhood organization in its aim to create a more Islamic society out of a conviction that developing the proper structures[12] will bring about a truly moral (but not totalitarian) Islamic society. Further, it has emphasized unity among Muslims and idealizes Palestinian unity, and eschews *takfir* (rejectionism, defining others as false Muslims), a key aspect of the ideology of radical salafis such as Osama bin Ladin. For many years, the Palestinian Muslim Brotherhood had put political activism on hold in Gaza, and focused instead on delivering religious and social services and missionary activity *(da`wa)*. This tactical strategy was necessary to ensure the Brotherhood's survival, as a result of the Egyptian government's severe suppression of the Brethren. Even when the Brethren were released from Egyptian jails, it was with the understanding that the group would not seek legal party status. The group's tactical approach in Gaza was to focus first on creating an Islamic social and political entity, for doing so, the group held, would eventually return Palestine to the Palestinians.[13]

Eventually, the founders of HAMAS developed a wing for militant action, thus breaking with the Palestinian, Egyptian, and Jordanian Muslim Brotherhood's more "movement-oriented" approach. HAMAS was then officially announced shortly after the outbreak of the First Intifadha. It gained support steadily in the population despite the signing of the Oslo Accords which the organization opposed, as did many other Palestinian factions and individuals. The suffering of much of the Palestinian population during the Oslo period, as well as the breakdown of Israeli-Palestinian negotiations, together with Ariel Sharon's incitement of Palestinians by insisting on bringing troops and signaling Israeli authority over the Haram al-Sharif—the compound containing the al-Aqsa Mosque and the Dome of the Rock that Israelis call the Temple Mount (to indicate the ruins of the Second Temple underneath the ground) in Jerusalem—led to the al-Aqsa or Second Intifadha. In this second popular uprising, HAMAS, as well as Fatah-linked organizations, engaged in militancy.

In the 1990s, HAMAS had become a refuge for many of those Palestinians who disagreed with the aims and leadership of the Oslo initiative. A substantial number of members of the Popular Committees of the PLO, the Popular Front for the Liberation of Palestine (PFLP) and the Democratic Front for the Liberation of Palestine (DFLP) also opposed Oslo, but these groups and HAMAS could agree on little other than continued resistance. The main thrust of HAMAS activities was not militant actions against Israel, but rather social, charitable, educational, and political programs aimed at Palestinians.

Civil society organizations delivering services and aid to the population have long been important in Palestinian camps and areas. Those created by the various arms of the PLO rivaled each other, and also to some extent the traditional elites in Palestinian society. HAMAS was also able to draw on the salience of religion in an Islamizing society. The number of mosques in Gaza doubled between 1967 and 1987. The Mujama` Islami model in Gaza established by Shaykh Yassin provided a different type of mosque community than the traditional one, offering affordable services and programs, often located within the mosques themselves.[14]

HAMAS also founded the Scientific Medical Association in 1997 which operated medical and dental services and a blood bank.[15] The group established the Association for Science and Culture, and provided education from kindergarten through eighth grade for Gazans. The Islamic Workers Union was set up in 1992. All of these efforts were extremely important, as were the creation of other educational bodies and the establishment of student blocs of support and organizations of professionals and women's associations which challenged some of the more secular-feminist orientation of other Palestinian groups.[16]

Especially after September 11, 2001 (9/11), U.S. advisors argued that a crackdown on HAMAS' charitable activities was of paramount importance. Dennis Ross and Matthew Levitt characterize the group's charitable and educational activities as nefarious efforts at recruitment, or to socialize new suicide bombers,[17] decrying the addition of "Koranic memorization centers" that "mimic in a religious setting the tight clique-like structure of the terrorist cell."[18] American and Israeli targeting of Muslim charitable or social organizations was not a novel policy. Israeli and American pressure had already been put on Arafat who closed more than 20 HAMAS organizations in 1997, and more closures took place in 2001 and 2002.[19] What was new, post-9/11, was an additional series of attacks on organizations thought to provide aid to HAMAS from abroad such as the Holy Land Foundation in the United States which was closed in 2001, but against which the government failed to secure a conviction in the Dallas-based trial which concluded in 2007.[20] The logic that the PA could replace the charitable and social services provided by HAMAS was faulty. It did not, but an important aim of HAMAS in 2004-05 was to reinstate some services to which it devotes the majority (something like 95 percent) of its annual budget.

Given the favorable perception of HAMAS, the negative perception of Arafat's clique-like leadership, and chaotic battles between youths loyal to different groups, as well as criminality and corruption, no one should have been surprised by HAMAS' electoral victory in 2006. At the time of this writing, the Israeli military and security sectors are in disaccord over the proper approach to the Palestinian population and HAMAS, despite a fragile truce engineered by external Arab states, which began June 19, 2008.

This monograph suggests that an understanding of the diverging paths of Israeli and HAMAS' strategic thought, along with an overview of HAMAS' development, explains the stand-off. Further, an understanding of the American role in the emergence of a regional security regime is useful. The United States can project power, aid deterrence, provide equipment, elicit cooperation, and provide formal and informal guarantees, thus its role seems essential in any solution to the current deadlock. However, the type of security regime that the United Status supports, such as the alliance between Israel and Mahmud Abbas' Fatah elements of the PA, may not necessarily be effective or durable, as Robert Lieber had suggested in a general analysis of the issue in the period following the first Gulf War.[21]

Disagreements within the Israeli military and political establishments over the national security objectives of that country reveal HAMAS' placement at the nexus of Israel's domestic, Palestinian, and regional objectives. This process can be traced back to Ariel Sharon's formation of the KADIMA Party, and the decision to withdraw unilaterally from Gaza without engaging in a peace process with Palestinians.

The reasons for this new strategy were: the assumption that it is unlikely that Arab armies would launch a conventional attack against Israel; fear of vulnerability within Israeli-held areas; and Israeli unwillingness to bargain with key Palestinian leadership (Arafat, the "new" Fatah as represented by imprisoned political figure Marwan Barghouti, or the Hamas leaders). It was now thought that Israel should hold to a defensive line encircling its citizens rather than holding on to Gaza and the West Bank for troop dispersal.[22] This new thinking comprised a defensive strategy that did not exactly replace, but stood alongside other Israeli approaches, for instance, that described by Yitzhak Shamir as aggressive defense, in other words, offensives aimed at creating security zones—in the south of Lebanon, notably to extend Israel's strategic depth.

The occupied territories had also been thought of as being valuable in land for peace negotiations, and during the Oslo process, according to one line of Israeli thought, Israel was ready to withdraw entirely in order to obtain peace.[23] Palestinians might argue that, in fact, Israel was never serious about this exchange, and its land-settlement policies during the Oslo period demonstrate this, as hundreds of settlements were established and/or expanded, and settlers were provided with various types of incentives, tax breaks, and other benefits. Settlers' safety, particularly in transit to and from the settlements, is an enormous headache for the Israeli authorities. Their resort to vigilante violence against Palestinians is an aspect of the conflict often overlooked in the Western media. Added to this lack of commitment was the failure of the parties to grapple with final status issues—Palestinian refugees, Jerusalem, etc. The optimism about negotiating and "Oslo expectations" faded with the al-Aqsa Intifadha, and Israelis blamed Palestinians for this failure, leading to claims and frequent statements from the Israeli Right and part of the Israeli Left that there was no "partner to peace."

Another segment of the Israeli Left has continued until this day to argue for land-for-peace and complete withdrawal from the territories. Still others recalculated the main threat as Palestinians who could, and did, threaten Israeli centers of population with suicide bombings, adding to that threat, the Palestinians living inside of Israel (Arab Israelis) who make up 20 percent of the population. Calls for their relocation or repatriation to the West Bank continue, and their employment, and that of Palestinians from the West Bank and Gaza, has been supplanted, Israeli policies against immigrant workers notwithstanding, by foreign non-Jewish immigrant workers.

According to Barry Rubin, the Israeli military felt the threat posed by Palestinians would not significantly increase, but that if settlers could be evacuated and a stronger line of defense erected, they could better defend their citizenry. That thinking led to the Wall or Security Fence. The remaining threat was missiles launched from Gaza, and indeed these continued. Israel claimed significant victories in its war against Palestinians by the use of targeted killings of leadership, boycotts, power cuts, etc., but also admitted that it had not "defeated the will to resistance."[24] Of course, this sentiment speaks directly to the ultimate challenge of all insurgencies in which the settler, or colonial, or invading power, essentially loses the war, if not specific battles, from the moment the resistance gains popular support.[25] And it shows that the situation might not be indefinitely manageable, and that Palestinians, despite every possible effort made to weaken, incriminate, and separate Arab allies from their interests, or pay collaborators, might yet edge Israelis—if they move away from their own politicians' and military's thinking—back toward comprehensive negotiations.

In a remarkable sequence of events, Fatah elements of the PA battled HAMAS and, despite the military training provided to them under U.S. auspices, they lost control of Gaza. The fratricidal 4-day conflict resulted in 80 fatalities; some were the settling of old scores, said Hanan Ashrawi, an independent Palestinian politician. Fatah and the al-Aqsa Martyrs Brigades carried out revenge actions, killing some, abducting some 23 persons, and attacking HAMAS-linked institutions in the West Bank. In a confusing move, thought to originate with U.S. advice but also with Israeli stances toward HAMAS in mind,[26] Mahmoud Abbas (whose supporters had lost the election, but who had been named to head the government because HAMAS wanted a unity government with Fatah) said he would dissolve his Cabinet, including Prime Minister Ismail Haniyeh of HAMAS, and that he would call for new elections. Haniyeh declared his intent to establish order in Gaza and called Abbas' decision hasty.[27]

HAMAS, which keeps only a token force in the West Bank, and does not admit its strength there, did not interfere with Abbas, but as his decision to replace Haniyeh with Salim Fayyad was illegal, Haniyeh is regarded as the Prime Minister of the PA by many Palestinians. The issue was that Abbas could dissolve the Cabinet, but had no constitutional right to appoint a new prime minister, or to dissolve the elected Parliament or call for new elections (which Israelis, Fatah, and perhaps Washington, hoped would undo the HAMAS' majority).

HAMAS set about restoring order in Gaza, and Abbas refused to recognize the HAMAS government there and, likewise, the Israelis and Americans speak only with his faction. Palestinians in Gaza then experienced an Israeli, American, and European cut-off of funds, then services, fuel, medicines, and finally food. The boycott on funds appeared to be a somewhat desperate attempt to cause Palestinians to overthrow HAMAS in Gaza in 2007. People began using cooking oil to drive automobiles and taxis, and were severely impacted by the boycott and closure.

Sieges abound in the history of warfare. The names of Jerusalem, Vienna, and Missalonghi come to mind. The idea of provoking a popular uprising has also recurred; unsuccessfully pursued by the British, French, and Israelis in the 1956 Suez (or Tripartite) War. Anthony Eden supposed the Egyptian population would overthrow President Jamal abd al-Nasir.

Ironically, the attacks cemented Nasir's popularity and vindicated his claims that the former colonial powers were conspiring with the new Zionist state they had helped establish. This time around, the *Jerusalem Post* trumpeted every action against HAMAS in Gaza and every instance of violence against Fatah, and many articles expressed fear of life in an Islamic state, which the *Post* calls "Hamasistan." Yet, the Gazan population did not overthrow their leadership.

All in all, HAMAS, after the initial, very regrettable violence in Gaza, restored order, and though continuing to battle certain powerful clans, earned respect; instituting the first "911" emergency telephone service, and operating more efficiently than expected, considering the boycott and the organized violence directed against it by the above-mentioned clans (like the Dughmush) and Fatah, both with external funding.[28] HAMAS discouraged the pro-Al-Qai'da groups operating in Gaza, although they did not have total control over the Islamic Army or Palestinian Islamic Jihad.

In February 2008, almost one-half of the 1.2 million Gazan population breached the Egyptian border to buy food and supplies that they had been denied for months under the Israeli boycott. This created a good deal of stress on the Israeli-Egyptian political relationship. Israel expected Egypt to moderate, even terminate its support for HAMAS; something that the Egyptian government could not do, given the strength of popular Egyptian support for HAMAS and the Palestinians trapped in Gaza. Israel (and also Washington) have maintained since that a condition of allowing the Rafah border to be opened would be for the Egyptians to pressure HAMAS from using the tunnels, allegedly used to bring arms into Gaza, although more recently to bring in food. Egypt agreed to dynamite the tunnels, but they remain an issue. Further, Israel wanted Egypt to pressure HAMAS to release Gilad Shalit. Shalit, an Israeli soldier, was captured in a raid on the Kerem Shalom crossing on June 25, 2006, by three armed groups, one of which was the Army of Islam. He was eventually transferred to HAMAS' custody, and the movement wants a prisoner exchange.

For months Israel steadfastly rejected diplomacy involving HAMAS and HAMAS' truce appeals as offered by Ismail Haniyeh early in 2008, but after efforts by Saudi Arabia and Qatar to mend the conflict between Fatah and HAMAS and a deal negotiated by Egypt, it entered into a temporary 6-month truce with HAMAS on June 19, 2008.[29]

Israel's greatest fear has been a united, properly coordinated and prepared Arab and Palestinian attack. Given Israel's rejection of all comprehensive peace offers by the Arabs and its forging and maintenance of separate agreements with Egypt and Jordan, it no longer fears such a coordinated attack by Palestinians and other Arab nations. It also seeks to prevent Palestinian factions from uniting and pursuing a full scale resistance as during the Al Aqsa Intifadha. Then actions coincided, although the factions were far from unified.

It has frequently been predicted that Israel should (and could) reconquer the Gaza strip, a rather futile overturning of its "new strategy," or, as suggested prior to HAMAS' electoral victory, engage the Palestinians in a war over the West Bank, or both. The "conflict-oriented" elements in Israel want it to engage in "preemptive deterrence" or attacks on other states in the region, perhaps Iran,[30] Lebanon[31] (because lack of preparation for the 2006 war was deemed the main issue), or Syria[32] in the longer term.

HAMAS' initial strategy of armed resistance and popular uprising against Israel has been tamed as it has instead pursued political participation, accepted the notion of a limited area of an envisioned Palestinian state, and in its calmings and truces which acknowledge (and therefore "recognize") Israel in a *de facto* manner.[33] It was severely criticized for this change in strategy by Ayman Zawahiri. Yet it continues to hold out the threat of popular resistance should negotiations fail and occupation continue, and is struggling militarily and politically against Fatah, its brother organization. Such civil strife is not HAMAS' preferred mode, and it has taken many unwanted steps and actions to seek an end to this strife which is fueled by external actors as well as internal divisions. HAMAS has put its vision of an Islamic state on hold as well as its general political stance of "positive versus negative freedom"[34]—tolerating, even recommending diversity and representation of other groups, if Palestinian autonomy can be pursued.

The underlying strategies of both Israel and HAMAS do not elicit strong optimism in a solution to the Israeli-Palestinian-Arab conflict, but each is still capable of revising its strategies, or desired end-states and establishing a long-term truce, or better yet, a longer-term peace.

A peaceful resolution to this conflict should remain a primary objective of Israel, the Palestinians, other Arab and Muslim nations, and of the United States. The Arab-Israeli conflict has complicated regional development in myriad ways, and remains a key grievance for a far broader Muslim population who see in it perfidy and hypocrisy by Israel, and that Israel's strongest ally, the United States, has not acted as a fair and neutral broker in affairs of the region.

If the next American president turns his attention to the Israeli-Palestinian conflict in a sustained, methodical, and creative manner together with other Quartet members and perhaps Arab delegates until resolution, then an important co-condition for success in the Global War on Terror will be achieved, as well as an enormous benefit to the citizens, economies, and political development of the region.

Summary of Recommendations.

A better understanding of HAMAS, its history and evolution, the reasons for and level of sympathies from Palestinians and other Muslim and Arab nations for the organization, and its stances on various issues is imperative for policymakers because the Islamist and nationalist base of support for the organization and its essential principles is not likely to disappear.

To the degree that the United States is committed to the establishment of a just and sovereign Palestinian entity, it would also behoove policymakers to consider carefully the ramifications of making alliances selectively with specific groups and actors in any society. The consequences of such alliances forged during the Saddam period with opposition groups can now be seen in Iraq, where the obvious "losers" in the new balance of power, Sunni Arabs, especially those with geographical and political links to the former regime, felt they had no stake in the new government. The Shi'i parties were supposed to include these groups in military and police structures but have not yet done so. In the Palestinian case, the current preferences for dealing with, or restricting U.S. support only to followers of Mahmud Abbas or members of his nonelected government in the West Bank have backfired, given the staying power of HAMAS. It would be best if these elements eventually chose to support a broader Palestinian alliance. Indeed, this is HAMAS' position, but it rests on a shift within the PA.

Meanwhile, more constructive policy avenues such as supporting the building of Palestinian institutions (with appropriate transparency[35]), aiding reform, and planning for the economic well-being of Palestinian society have taken a backseat to 2006 and 2007 actions intended to strangle HAMAS, all of which were ineffective, or thus far, destructive. Some similarities with the South African and Irish situations are instructive.[36] The violence, while not symmetrical, has gone so far as to injure the moral standing of both parties—Israelis and Palestinians (associated with HAMAS, Palestinian Islamic Jihad [PIJ], and certain other groups) even if national survival is at stake. Yet, in the Irish case, negotiators included the Sinn Fein; and in the South African case, the previously violent actions of the African National Congress were permitted to recede into the past so that a new society, free of racial injustice, could be established.

The first course of action that I had recommended in January 2008 was to accept the offer of Ismail Haniyeh to a restored truce. The temporary truce concluded on June 17, 2008, was therefore an important first step.

A much more significant prisoner exchange needs to take place. Fewer than 500 of the 10,000 Palestinian political prisoners were released in 2006-07. Palestinians should prevail on HAMAS to release Shalit as an act of good faith. HAMAS, however, is adamant that a substantial number of its prisoners be released in the exchange.[37] The Israeli and international boycott of the PA government is also supposed to end under the current truce, and this is absolutely essential to restore key services, medicines, foods, and reprovide salaries. HAMAS' and other charitable social services which have been attacked in the West Bank must be put back under professional management. There is no reason for them to operate as Fatah, rather than as HAMAS' entities. However, they can and must do so with the greatest degree of transparency,[38] as should town *zakat* committees, which are a very important source of social welfare.

Israel needs to abandon the aspects of its new defensive strategy which are calculated to thwart peace efforts. Reliance on perimeter control as through barriers has, along with years of constricting movement, curfews, and land acquisition policies, led to a terrible apartheid-like separation of the population and threatens any coherence to the West Bank. It may be impossible to convince Israel to dismantle the security fence, known as the Wall. But there would be a great benefit to doing so. The Jewish and Palestinian populations do not need to be herded into separate areas—they need to be reacquainted with each other, as segregation has bred hatred and fear. Further, the Israeli military's desire to engage in limited partial and temporary withdrawals, followed by territorial reconquests is antithetical to conflict resolution as it destroys the prospect of trust.

As a HAMAS spokesperson stated: "We are not against trust or security. We know the Israelis would like to have security. . . but at the same time, we know we cannot live with our own liquidation." To the same degree, when HAMAS reserves the option of reengaging in violent jihad, the trust that must—if there is to be peace—be extended by Israelis is eroded. A long-term truce must be safe for all, honorable, bring justice, and a remedy to the Palestinians who have been deprived their self-determination and their freedom, but also ensure an end to violence.

The deepest challenge to HAMAS is that, in return for territory, it must abandon the strategy of militant resistance and focus on supplying good governance. It will need to uncouple the dream of martyrdom from nationalist violence, for its own cadres and other youth. That may only be accomplished, given the religious strictures around jihad that HAMAS recognizes through the device of a long-term truce, but that truce would be desirable.

The world community should discourage Israel from enacting further restrictions on Palestinians that will prevent them from working inside of Israel. This has debased both the Israeli national conception of its citizens and further transformed Gaza and the West Bank into Bantustans, confining a population which used to work inside of Israel. An economic and developmental solution needs the input of all parties, in addition to the political/military situation, so that Palestinians do not live in closed areas devoid of sufficient employment, or food and goods, as prompted the flight to Egypt in early 2008. A return to the more hopeful planning of a Palestinian state, as evinced in several studies,[39] is required. In the last years, the United States shifted its emphasis toward state-building in the Middle East to Iraq, and secondarily to Afghanistan, necessarily so. However, it has not been wise to diminish its peace efforts to symbolic exchanges of good intent with select factions of the Palestinians and Israelis (while sponsoring a "Contra-like" action against HAMAS under supporters of Muhammad Dahlan and other Fatah elements). U.S. foreign policy in the Middle East would be greatly strengthened with an *entente* between Israel and all of the Palestinians.

While this should eventually determine "final status" compromises, it need not do so at present, as Haim Malka has recommended, but reentering a phase of negotiating—with all parties, including HAMAS—is essential. (Should negotiations falter, he then recommends a unilateral Israeli withdrawal from the West Bank.)[40] Palestinians, even Ahmed Qurei, and Sari Nusseibeh, have stated that there is a limited window for negotiations now, and each have suggested a return to the notion of a one-state solution, which I believe would be disastrous for the Palestinians.

Background.

HAMAS, meaning zeal or enthusiasm (an acronym for Harakat al-Muqawama al-Islamiyya or the Movement of the Islamic Resistance), is an offshoot of the Islamist trend in Palestinian society. HAMAS' origins are with the Palestinian branch of the Muslim Brotherhood movement (referred to as Ikhwan or Brethren) which dates back to the 1940s, and the Egyptian parent branch which dates back to 1928. However, it should also be noted that Fatah (the largest of the four organizations of the PLO) was not exclusively or particularly secularist. Indeed, the founding members of Fatah, with the exception of Yasir Arafat, were all members of the Muslim Brotherhood organization, which later produced HAMAS.

HAMAS' rather late emergence evolved from Israel's antagonism to Palestians and the necessarily quiescent policies of the Muslim Brotherhood toward both Egypt and Jordan. The Muslim Brotherhood was challenged by the Saraya al-Jihad al-Islami, or Palestinian Islamic Jihad, which emerged in the early

1980s and began to attract the support of Palestinian youth. Clearly, other reasons for popular support for a new type of Palestinian resistance movement can also be traced to the exodus of the PLO leadership to Lebanon from 1967-70 and its forced retreat to Tunis, following the 1982 Israeli invasion of Lebanon. This distant leadership reacted to, rather than led, grass-roots developments like the First Intifadha in the Palestinian occupied territories.

Other important reasons for the emergence of HAMAS (and Islamic Jihad and other Islamist actors like the Islamic Movement inside Israel and smaller salafist organizations) were the worsening economic conditions in the territories, and the effect of Israel's counterinsurgent measures taken first against the PLO and later against all other forms of Palestinian political, cultural, intellectual, and militant associations and activities. The heightening of Islamist sentiment in the Middle East as in Palestinian communities in exile has only increased since HAMAS' official establishment in 1987.

Some accounts simply describe HAMAS emerging from the previously-mentioned organization called the Mujama` Islami established by Shaykh Ahmed Yasin, who became an extremely popular preacher and scholar upon his return to Gaza from Egypt. One account links two paramilitary organizations, a Security Section (Jihaz al-Amn) and al-Mujahidun al-Falastiniyun (which included the Izz al-Din Qassam brigades), directly to Shaykh Yasin.[41] In fact, the rationale and preparations for militant activities against the Israeli occupation of the West Bank and Gaza date to the late 1970s as Yasin and others believed that the "jihad as *da`wa*" must be complemented with jihad as armed struggle.

Earlier the Brotherhood had decided not to support Khalil al-Wazir's initial suggestion in 1957 to form a group to liberate Palestine.[42] Certain individuals went ahead anyway and formed the Palestine National Liberation Movement, Fatah. Fatah's belief was that a national liberation movement would impel the Arab armies to fight for the Palestinian cause. President Jamal abd al-Nasir of Egypt, a highly popular figure in the Arab world, had suppressed the Muslim Brotherhood following an alleged assassination attempt on him in 1956. Nasir was supported by Palestinians for his commitment to Arab nationalism and unity. Yet, like King Husayn of Jordan, his aims were not identical with Palestinians' guerrilla efforts, which elicited sharp Israeli responses and military attacks.

The 1967 defeat of the Arab armies showed the disappointing result of Palestinian reliance on Arab governments and militaries as far as many were concerned, among them Shaykh Yasin. He was convinced that Palestinians must mount their own resistance, and began focusing on cadre formation, participation in, and organization of demonstrations and strikes. A conference was held in Amman in 1983 at which time a decision was made to support jihad by the Ikhwan in Palestine. Simultaneously, $70,000 raised by the Kuwaiti branch of the Ikhwan was received by the Palestine Committee (also known as the Inside Committee).[43] Various committees were established by Palestinian Ikhwan from Jordan, Saudi Arabia, and other Gulf states to support the resolutions taken in Amman, and within a few years, a body, the Jihaz Falastin (Palestine Apparatus), was in operation.

Meanwhile, Shaykh Yasin began buying arms, mainly from the Israeli black market, but was stung by Israeli collaborators. Those involved were caught, tortured by Israelis, and revealed the network up to Shaykh Yasin, who was arrested and put on trial in 1984.[44] The Israelis found about half of the weapons purchased; the others were hidden. Yasin was released from jail in the Ahmad Jibril prisoner exchange in 1985.[45] The entire incident bolstered those Ikhwan, particularly in the West Bank, who had maintained that armed jihad against Israel, as a local initiative, would fail, and that the correct path was to continue working toward an Islamic state.

However, the movement acquired martyrs during a 1986 protest at Bir Zeit University and became increasingly popular and participatory in public events. During the Intifadha, the *`Amn* (or security arm of HAMAS) became active and went after Israeli collaborators in squads known as the Majd. These in turn also embarked on armed actions against the Israelis after the Intifadha began in 1987.

HAMAS was announced shortly after the outbreak of the Intifadha on December 14, 1987, though it made December 8, 1987, its official date of establishment to coincide with the Intifadha.[46] Its founders included Shaykh Ahmad Yasin; Salah Shahadah, a former student leader who headed the military wing; Muhammad Sha`ah; Abd al-`Aziz Rantisi, a physician at the Islamic University; `Isa al-Nashar; Ibrahim al-Yazuri; Abd al-Fattah Dukhan; and Yahya al-Sinuwwar.

Postponement of Militant Islamism?

As explained above, HAMAS and the Islamic trend emerged more belatedly than in other parts of the Muslim world due to Palestinian dislocation and the struggle against Israel. When those secular Palestinians committed to armed resistance were essentially neutralized with their exile from Lebanon and moved towards negotiation, other ordinary Palestinians were greatly disappointed by the peace negotiation process. They instead arrived at a new commitment to armed resistance so long as Israel opposed the return of territory and sovereignty to Palestinians. This elided with the populism and support for resistance that was expressed in the Intifadha.

Decades earlier, a small militant Palestinian Islamist group was led by `Izz al-Din al-Qassam (1882-1935) who was killed in Jenin by the British, although his followers, the Qassamiyun, continued to fight in the Great Uprising of 1936-39.[47] HAMAS named its own military wing after this proto-revolutionary movement.

A transregional emergence of similar groups in the region appeared by the late 1970s. However, the growth of viable political institutions in general was inhibited among Palestinians because of their status as a people without a state and the tight security controls imposed by Israel on the population. These, on the one hand, meant close surveillance and frequent detentions or arrests of Palestinians. At the same time, Israel's attacks on Palestinians, land policies, and extreme restrictions on movements, communications, publication, education, and all aspects of normal life which were intended to protect the Israeli population inspired first the guerrilla-style attacks of the *fida'iyin* and the more secular nationalist PLO.

The Muslim Brotherhood referred to above was established in Egypt in 1928 by Hasan al-Banna, a schoolteacher who believed that Muslims, particularly their youth, required a force for unity, aid, development, and education, and should take a direction other than that proposed by nationalist elites. The Brethren (Ikhwan) set up branches in Syria, the Sudan, Libya, the Gulf states, Jordan (which influenced the West Bank), and Gaza. From 1948 through the 1950s, military rule over the Palestinians was sufficiently repressive, and the Brothers both there and within Egypt were under siege, either underground or put in prison by the Nasir regime, or in exile. For 2 decades, the Palestinian Muslim Brotherhood focused on its religious, educational, and social missions, and was quiescent politically. That changed with the 1987 (First) Intifadha also known as the *intifadha* of stones, because the Palestinians were primarily reacting to Israeli force in demonstrations by throwing stones and burning tires. However, the outburst of popular resistance even in the face of constant and numerous arrests, collective punishments, destruction of property, and other punitive actions, and Israel's use of live ammunition against children armed with stones, along with the new use of videos, made Israel subject to international condemnation. This sort of condemnation, emanating more strongly from Europe than the United States, was unlike any it had faced in countering militant attacks of the Palestinian fighters over the border in Lebanon, or as the target of terrorist aircraft hijackings in the period from 1969 to about 1974.

The Muslim Brotherhood had advocated *da'wa,* which is the reform and Islamization of society and thought; *`adala* (social justice); and an emphasis on *hakimiyya* (the sovereignty of God, as opposed to temporal rule). Due to the severe repression of the Muslim Brotherhood in both Egypt and Jordan, the Palestinian Ikhwan were influenced, or even restrained by the parent organization, to support *da`wa* rather than militant jihad (or jihad by the sword[48]). HAMAS broke with the previous tactical thinking of the Palestinian

Muslim Brotherhood in an important way when it turned to armed resistance against Israel.

Islamic Jihad.

The Ikhwan were at first sidelined both by the spontaneous activism of Palestinians of various backgrounds (PLO and other) and by Islamic Jihad which had accelerated its operations in 1986 and 1987. *Harakat al-Jihad al-Islami fi Filastin* (The Movement of Islamic Jihad in Palestine, known as PIJ) was established by Fathi Shiqaqi, Shaykh `Abd al-`Aziz al-`Awda, and others, including current director general Ramadan Abdullah Shallah, in the Gaza Strip in the 1970s following their acceptance in Egypt of an Islamist vision similar to the Egyptian Muslim Brotherhood. However, these Palestinians distinguished themselves from secular nationalists and antinationalist Islamists in calling for grassroots organization and armed jihad to liberate Palestine as part of the Islamic solution.[49] The PIJ military apparatus known as Saraya al-Quds (Jerusalem Brigades) was operative by 1985, and attacked Israeli military at an induction ceremony in 1986 known as the Gate of Moors operation. Palestinian youth, who were both territorially and generationally neglected by the PLO leadership that had been forcibly moved to Tunis, admired the militance of this group.

HAMAS' Growth.

Yasin's successful institutionalization through the Mujama` Islami, fundraising and *da`wa* via the earlier established Jam`iyah Islamiyah (1967) funded HAMAS' growth. In Gaza, where the Muslim Brothers had less prestige in some ways than other Palestinian thinkers,

Yasin reprinted the last volume of Sayyid Qutb's monumental *Fi Dhilal al-Qur'an*, a nontraditional *tafsir*, or explanation and interpretation of the "art" of the Quran, with funds from the Jam`iyah. In this way, he was able to introduce Qutb (d. 1966) now known in the West primarily as a "radical" martyr, executed by Egypt's President Nasir, as a "revolutionary fighting for justice and as a scholar of the highest standing"[50] because of the subject matter (the study of the Qur'an) and his sophisticated treatment. The Mujama`/ mosque-building/charitable phase of HAMAS was also successful due to its international connections.

The Muslim Brotherhood in Jordan was able to deliver aid from Arab countries and scholarships for promising students.[51] While the Israelis were cracking down on the PLO, religious and charitable organizations in the occupied territories encountered somewhat less interference until 1977. The number of mosques under Ikhwan authority doubled and offered kindergartens, Qur'an classes, and free circumcisions on certain days. The Ikhwan paid for the accompanying celebrations for circumcisions, and mobile medical units provided low cost or free services.[52] As described above, HAMAS moved actively into the areas of labor representation, education, professional associations, and throughout all sectors of Palestinian society in Gaza and also in the West Bank.

Various figures and their connections with the Ikhwan in Egypt were key to HAMAS' emergence, and so, too, was the degree of repression inside Israeli jails. Israeli journalist Amira Hass writes that "tens of thousands of Palestinians came to know Israelis through the experience of prisons and detention camps."[53] Palestinians were often held for 2 to 4 months or more without being charged, and were subjected to harsh interrogations, including torture.[54] As prisoners tried to unite to obtain radios, legally mandated visits, and then later other concessions by going on hunger strikes since 1971, the Israeli authorities first physically separated them in different locations, and, later, more effectively divided them by providing employment within prison to some but not others. The Islamization of Palestinian society ongoing outside of the prison walls began to be replicated inside as well.

The impetus to opposition was fostered in a different way by the nationalist-religious Israeli coalition in power from 1977. This government promoted settlement activity in the West Bank among which a Jewish group with extreme messianic views, the Gush Emunim, were important. One focus of such right wing groups was on symbols of Judaism, and new sources of conflict erupted where these symbols conflicted with Muslim claims, for instance at the Haram al-Sharif, or Temple Mount site in Jerusalem; the Haram al-Ibrahimi mosque in Hebron; and elsewhere. Two Muslims were killed in 1982 at the Haram al-Sharif, and a group tried to blow up the site in 1984. Another Jewish group threatened to destroy other Muslim shrines, and two students were murdered at the Islamic University of Hebron.[55] This caused more identification with religious-nationalist causes, certainly seen later after the massacre of Muslims at the al-Ibrahimi mosque, which sparked HAMAS' first suicide attacks, and when Ariel Sharon brought troops onto the Haram al-Sharif.

The Palestinian diaspora was also affected by the growth of the new Islamist thinking. The Palestinian Ikhwan student movement in Kuwait was inspired by such non-Ikhwan figures as Shaykh Hasan Ayyub.[56] Palestinian politics have played out in student movements featuring strong factionalism between Fatah and the Popular Committees, for instance, and it was in this period that the Islamic trend emerged, no longer tolerating suppression by Fatah supporters.

The General Union of Palestinian Students (GUPS) was represented at Kuwait University. GUPS had been wholly Fatah in orientation (not only because Fatah's formative body came from Kuwait). Nonetheless, a student group formed under the name al-Haqq, which included Khalid Mish`al, tried to influence GUPS concerning the impact of President Sadat's visit to Israel and the Lebanese civil war's impact on Palestinians.[57] The students saw these events to be crucial in that Israel was successfully forcing a wedge between the Palestinians and portions of their Arab support. Al-Haqq eventually went its own way as the Islamic Association of Palestinian Students. Similar organizations in the United Kingdom (UK) and the United States formed in the early 1980s.

Another important nucleus for HAMAS was at the Islamic University in Gaza, founded mostly by Ikhwan members associated with Shaykh Yasin's al-Mujam`a al-Islami in 1978. The University, backed by Arafat, enabled the Ikhwan in mobilization as the institution educated thousands of Palestinians from an Islamic viewpoint. It became even more important with the outbreak of the First Intifadha.

Points of Doctrine.

When HAMAS was established, it defined its mission as the liberation of Palestinians and cessation of Israeli aggression against them. That is to say, its goal is **not** the destruction of Israel,[58] as is commonly asserted by the American and Israel media, and certainly HAMAS does not possess the military means to attain that goal.

In February 1988, the Brotherhood granted formal recognition to HAMAS as a result of a key meeting in Amman, Jordan, involving the spiritual guide of the Jordanian Muslim Brotherhood, Shaykh Abd al-Rahman al-Khalifa; Ibrahim Ghosheh, the HAMAS spokesperson and Jordanian representative; Mahmud Zahar, a surgeon; al-Rantisi, a West Bank representative; Jordanian parliament members; and the hospital director. In 1988, HAMAS issued its now infamous Charter, which it no longer cites or refers to. This document condemns world Zionism and the efforts to isolate Palestine, and has been exhaustively discussed by scholar Andrea Nüsse along with HAMAS' ideas as expressed in *Filastin al-Muslima*, a journal produced outside of the territories.[59] Another important source of HAMAS' positions and ideas is to be found in its *bayanat* (bayans or official announcements) which, unlike the journal, come from within the occupied territories and illustrate the centrality of the First Intifadha to the emerging HAMAS. Other earlier comprehensive presentations of HAMAS' ideas are explained in academic publications. Some of HAMAS' earlier ideas which remain relevant have now undergone significant change or nuance. These are:

- HAMAS will bring about a return to the true Islam. (This implies an evolution carried out by Islamists rather than the "return" to the past.) However, the nationalist struggle for the fatherland (*watan*) is an integral part of the path toward the true Islam. An Islamic state in Palestine will be a victory for the entire Muslim *ummah*.[60]
- HAMAS is the true heir of the historic Islamist Shaykh Qassam movement because it is populist

(and militant), in contrast with the ineffective, compromising politics of the Palestinian elite.[61]

- Israel was entrenching itself and its land-grabbing policies with the wave of Soviet immigration that brought about one million new Jewish immigrants to Israel.[62]
- HAMAS, despite the claim of brotherhood in the nationalist struggle, disputed the PLO's right to solely represent the Palestinian people. It adopted an argument made by many, including Ziad Abu Amr, that indicts the hierarchical PLO leadership and its disconnect with the territories.[63]

The Charter, which was the first written effort to express HAMAS' goals, was issued in 1988 and has been sharply criticized for its anti-Jewish and anti-Zionist statements. It incorporates Hasan al-Banna's statement that Israel would eventually be swept away (as other nations have risen and fallen before it).

Khalid Mish`al, the current leader of HAMAS, claims that the Charter "should not be regarded as the fundamental ideological frame of reference from which the movement takes its positions."[64] And another important HAMAS leader, Ibrahim Ghosheh, has explained that the Charter is "not sacred," its articles are "subject to review."[65] More important than the Charter to our analysis might be the HAMAS document, "This is What We Struggle For,"[66] or the document, *The Islamic Resistance Movement* issued in 2000.[67]

The latter traces HAMAS' history, expressing the view that the Palestinian people's role, particularly a military role, is central to the struggle. In contrast, the role of Arab governments has decreased ever since the defeat of their armies in 1967. The past experiences of the Ikhwan both in military and *da`wa* activities are outlined, along with the historical phases of HAMAS. The movement has rejected negotiation with Israel (in contrast to the PLO) and garnered opposition in the post-Oslo period as it retaliated against Israel for that country's assassination of Yahya Ayash. Yet HAMAS has adapted strategically and politically.

Its defined enemy is the Zionist Project (not Jews), and it believes that liberation of Palestine depends on a Palestinian, Arab, and Islamic circle.[68] That liberation will be accomplished by military means, but "civilian Zionists" are not targets, only "military Zionists" are. However, civilians might "inadvertently be hit or may be targeted only in retaliation for the enemy's targeting of Palestinian civilians."[69]

HAMAS also expressed ambiguity toward the West generally, and the United States because of its unquestioning and seemingly unconditional support to Israel. For some years, HAMAS' journal also included articles about Western fears of Islam (what is now called Islamophobia). These, they maintained, had arisen from a certain historical arrogance whereby the West rejected the idea that Islam formed the basis for Western civilization.[70] At one time, it would not have been necessary to explain that Islamic civilization expressed a commitment religiously and legally to the monotheism shared with "the West" (Christianity and Judaism); political ideas of the perfect society and form of rule inspired by Plato; and that it was a well of synthesis, in which Hellenic, Byzantine, Arab, Persian, Indian, and other intellectual, cultural, artistic, scientific, mathematical, and medical progress was made while Europe was in the "Dark Ages." It was transmitted "back" to the West in translations of the Arabic works of Avicenna (Ibn Sina, who influenced St. Thomas Aquinas) and Averroes (Ibn Rushd). This idea, by the way, is not an Islamist eccentricity; the great historian Marshall Hodgson wrote that in conceptualizing world history, one could divide the world into four parts, and that Europe, or the West, and the Middle East were closest in their philosophical influences, monotheism, and culture (the Muslim scholars developed and gone beyond the Hellenic and Indic legacies).[71]

Islamists have long accepted the principles of the French Revolution,[72] but view the West's lack of support for democratization where Islamists were strong, or prevailed as in Algeria, Egypt, and Palestine after 2006, as hypocritical. HAMAS, then and now, denies the clash of civilization thesis that became more well-known through Samuel Huntington, and also—importantly—the Al-Qa'idist proposal that Muslims must wage jihad against the West.

HAMAS has also been accused of seeking to impose an Islamic order in which Arab Christians would be second-class citizens, as would women. Clashes concerning behavior, and what we could call a vigilante reaction by HAMAS cadres, did take place against bars and wine shops owned by Christians and, years previously, in attacks by youth on women not wearing hijab or when in April 2005 gunmen killed a woman in her fiance's car and beat him, which greatly "embarrased the HAMAS leadership," which decried these incidents.[73] These actions undercut the leadership's position that it respected and protected women and minorities, its argument that Palestinian Christians are as poorly treated by Israelis as Palestinian Muslims,[74] and that Palestinian unity is required.

By 2004, lower-level cadres' fervor against bars and wine shops had been replaced with a policy of actively protecting Christian residents of Ramallah, and including them on HAMAS political lists.[75] After HAMAS' take-over of Gaza, order was imposed on salafist groups who had more extreme views, like the Army of Islam.

With HAMAS' electoral victory, media interest in Christian and women's reactions was kindled, and showed that some prominent Palestinian Christians are justifiably uncomfortable with the historical concept of the *ahl al-dhimma,* the protected minorities under an Islamic state,[76] or with Islamist stances on public virtue and morality. But HAMAS' constant assertion is that Islamic rule will not be forced on Palestinians.[77] Christians were supported by HAMAS in Ramallah, for example. And although the *hijab* is ubiquitous in Gaza, some women claim they feel secure moving around without it.

The only woman in the HAMAS' formed cabinet was, predictably, the Minister of Women's Affairs, Myriam Saleh, who has stated:

> We assure all women that we will not force anybody to wear the hijab . . . we only present our ideas by suggestion and with good intention. The majority of Palestinian women wear the hijab with full conviction and without coercion from anyone.[78]

Much more could be said about the competition between HAMAS-sponsored women's organizations and those that emerged from the other "secularist" or Left elements of the PLO. However, HAMAS and its female representatives have produced a more mature discourse as time has gone on,[79] in a way not dissimilar to Hizbullah's approach to women's issues.

Relations with the PLO-Fatah and the Peace Processes.

During the course of the first Intifadha, more Palestinians than ever before severed ties with Israel to the degree that they could. This went along with a call for self-sufficiency as with "Intifadha farms," raising produce, chickens, and dairy cows, and boycotting Israeli products, refusing to pay taxes, and in merchants' closing of their stores. HAMAS' pragmatism in limiting some of these demands on the population was paralleled in its limited and calculated use of jihad. As the Madrid peace conference of 1991 was held, HAMAS' military activity increased. This reoccurred when Israelis killed Palestinian civilians (the circumstance that HAMAS rationalizes as *fard `ayn;* that is, when jihad becomes a requisite individual duty) and when, to punish HAMAS for kidnapping and killing a border policemen, Israeli officials deported 415 HAMAS and Islamic Jihad activists to Lebanon in December 1992, including leaders like Abd al-Aziz Rantisi.

Israel had wanted to decrease HAMAS' recruitment successes within the prison system by exiling these prisoners, and it hoped to do so permanently. The move backfired, as it brought world attention to the violation of international law and the human rights of the activists, who were stranded on the southern Lebanese hillside of Marj al-Zuhur. There, instead of being isolated in Israeli prisons, they received visits from journalists, dignitaries, and Fatah representatives.[80] The deportation also sparked HAMAS' leaders in Jordan to carry out attacks, and more activity centered in the West Bank.

According to some, the deportation followed an agreement between HAMAS and Iran.[81] The Iranians were unhappy with Arafat's détente with Israel and had, in fact, attacked the PLO offices in Tehran. However, the degree of any Iranian relationship with HAMAS is greatly disputed. Israelis claim large-scale Iranian military and material support for HAMAS from Iran, but others point only to visits to Iran by HAMAS and expressions of solidarity.

Oslo.

When the news of the Oslo Agreements broke, which essentially ended the first Intifadha, the situation became much more difficult for HAMAS. Their principles stated that the PLO could not any more claim to be the sole representative of the Palestinian people, and thus had no right to enter into negotiations with Israel without an indicator of the popular will. Further, they, like Khalid Mish`al, hold that it is not up to Israel or the United States to force Palestinians to recognize and submit to occupation via a "recognition" of Israel which amounted to an acceptance of Zionism.[82] HAMAS tried unsuccessfully to unify those opposed to Oslo and determined to continue its jihad. That meant both dissension and negotiation with the PLO as it took on the PA and was pressed by Israel to contain violence.

Over time, especially as the peace process faltered, there was increasing strife between Fatah and HAMAS. At the same time, ordinary Palestinians began to support HAMAS more strongly as the PA failed to provide substantive and positive gains to show for the trading of land and principles.

By January 2006, HAMAS won a majority in the PA's general legislative elections. This advent brought condemnation from Israel and ensued in a power struggle carried out in several stages with PA President Mahmud Abbas and the Fatah party. The United States, which has included HAMAS on an official list of terrorist organizations for some years, and the European Union (EU) boycotted the PA even though HAMAS established a power-sharing government with Fatah by accepting Abbas' presidency. The Palestinian population and government were cut off from much-needed funds and services like electricity which are paid and distributed through Israel. Meanwhile, various Fatah leaders, like Muhammad Dahlan, were funded and supported to engage in violence against HAMAS.[83] Restrictions were placed on travel by HAMAS' leaders like Isma'il Haniya, who had toured Arab and world capitals and raised funds in the post-election period. Haniya was forced to leave all the funds he had raised behind at the Egyptian border when he returned to Gaza. Israeli military attacks continued on Gaza, despite its status of "disengagement." HAMAS had to confront Dahlan, this force, and other PA fighters, the government went without salaries, and the population was cut off from aid.

A media campaign that continues to the present was waged against HAMAS in the West and in the Israeli press. Israel's hope was that the resulting chaos would reestablish Fatah's control over leadership. But apparently more than media efforts were waged against HAMAS. It appears that a "soft coup" was planned, and that forces loyal to President Mahmoud Abbas were to be strengthened at the same time as HAMAS was to be weakened. News of this plan appeared in the Arab press at the end of April 2007 in a disputed document implicating a faction within the U.S. administration and "Arabs (Egyptian and Jordanian)" who plotted to bolster Abbas to the detriment of HAMAS in the wake of the Mecca Agreement, forged between HAMAS and Fatah, and its breakdown.[84] This supported the Arab view that the United States had opposed Saudi Arabia's initiative taken to end fratricide between HAMAS and Fatah.

Finally, these events led to HAMAS' decision to preempt Dahlan's and Abbas' efforts, in which it routed the Fatah forces in Gaza in battles fought on June 13-14, 2007. Battles also took place in the West Bank. Forgotten was the fact that HAMAS had been legitimately elected but had agreed to a national unity government. To punish them, Abbas "fired" HAMAS' prime minister, declaring his intent to install a new (Fatah) government instead of the 3-month-old national unity government.[85] The result was two governments, one HAMAS-run in Gaza, and the other under Abbas in the West Bank, although HAMAS is strong enough to challenge Fatah's authority in the West Bank should it wish to do so. HAMAS' position was that it would seek national unity despite the unfair policies against it.

Ziad Abu Amr explained the struggle in this way: "If you have two brothers, put them into a cage, and deprive them of basic essential needs for life; they will fight."[86] The struggle has in some ways simplified, but in other ways complicated, Israel's approach to HAMAS. It refuses categorically to negotiate with HAMAS and meets exclusively with Abbas' Fatah-drawn government. But this situation cannot continue if there is to be any successful negotiation of the broader conflict.

Revolutionary Resistance vs. Overwhelming Force (Means).

Israeli aircraft bombed the building where Ahmad Yasin was staying in September 2003, and 6 months later on March 22, 2004, an Israeli helicopter gunship fired air-to-ground *Hellfire* missiles at him as he was being wheeled out of an early morning prayer service, killing eight others, and injuring another dozen people. The international community condemned the assassination; however, Ariel Sharon had directly approved the orders to kill Yasin. Thousands protested;[87] however, the policy of targeted killings continued with al-Rantisi's death on April 17, 2004, and with the deaths of other HAMAS leaders.

Israeli authorities did not distinguish between HAMAS' carefully separated political and military wings, consequently many HAMAS moderates were killed or jailed along with those who could be caught in the secret military wing. However, it was well-known that the political and military wings of HAMAS had long since been separated and were sufficiently independent of each other as to adopt very different political positions. For example, they clashed over the benefit of political participation when the opportunity first presented itself in 1996, and some HAMAS figures ran as independents.[88]

HAMAS' use of violence is its response to what it sees as state terror on the part of Israel. For that reason, it allowed attacks on Israeli military, but not on civilians in acts of revenge. This principle fell apart with the advent of suicide bombings, often an individual, self-recruited action. HAMAS has disallowed such actions during truces, although some other Palestinian groups have enacted them.

In summary, what is needed is to alter both the means employed and the ends sought of both sides in the conflict.

Ends.

Neither Israel nor the Palestinians have a unified position towards the other. Each group is socialized in particular ways, through the educational system, employment experiences; and for Israelis, in the military, in political parties, families, and bureaucracies. To understand the divergent views of the conflict and how each "side" views its goals or ends, one must look more deeply within the two communities.

According to Israeli sociologist Baruch Kimmerling, Israelis had an image of themselves as a unified society under an earlier Zionist self-sacrificing, land-working vision. This vision is no longer accurate, and today he describes seven cultures, all of which have been impacted by the increasing role of religion and militarism. These seven cultures are: "the previously hegemonic secular Askhenazi upper middle class, the national religious [ultra-religious who are nationalists], the traditionalist Mizrahim (Orientals) [meaning Jews from the broader Middle East, Central Asia, India], the Orthodox religious, the Arabs, the new Russian immigrants, and the Ethiopians."[89] A cultural code of Jewishness (ranging from very devout to aetheistic) and a nonsecular system are the only commonality for six of these groupings, and there are distinct limits to Israel's democracy as Arabs have no real legitimacy in this schema. Security, Kimmerling contends, has become a civil religion in Israel, signaling the subordination of the nonmilitary to the military. And within the six Jewish cultures, he sees three different orientations to the "enemy" (Arabs and Muslims), these being securitist (*bitchonist*), conflict-oriented, and compromise or peace-oriented.[90]

The securitist view is that Israel would be doomed by a major military defeat. The state owes the Israeli people security from this fate. Both war- and peacemaking are functions belonging to the military, according to this way of thinking. The conflict-oriented (who differ slightly from the *bitchonistim*) aim to retain as much land as possible of historic/Biblical Israel for moral and religious, and not just security reasons. These groups include those who want a complete elimination of a Palestinian threat, whether by permanent conquest and deportation, relocation, or other dispersal of Palestinians living where, in their view, Jews should live. But securitists also include those who can conceive of a PA which accepts Israel's security needs. To both securitists and the conflict-oriented, "security" refers to demographic challenge as much as violence. Compromise-oriented Israelis see that a peace in which Israel was accepted in the region would provide security. Hence, Israel's desired end-state(s): free of enemies, free of non-Jews, democratic yet halakhic (following Jewish law) are all but unachievable, and are disputed between the three security orientations that cut across its polyglot culture. Of the three, it is the compromise-oriented who are most willing to, or who have already called for, dialogue with HAMAS.

All of this means that the Israeli security culture is not exactly like that in the United States, nor is the Palestinian "security culture" if we can hypothesize one under occupation, and without sovereignty. When the United States seemingly borrows from Israeli military and counterterrorist policies, as it has been accused of doing in Iraq,[91] there are nevertheless certain qualitatively different assumptions that hold, even if the defensive framework (a defense against global terror) takes shape in policies that break with, for instance, the notion of "clean arms" or not attacking civilians.[92] Mira Sucharov has shown how Israel has developed a defensive security ethic (part of its security culture) but continuously pursued an offensive security doctrine.[93] If this is not a paradox, then it may not be so difficult to perceive HAMAS' intention of defending Muslims, through the means of jihad if necessary, even though this is not a symmetrical struggle or exact mirror image.

HAMAS' goal is the liberation of Palestine (not destruction of the Jews), and its "frame of reference" is Islam.[94] HAMAS does aim to create a more Islamic society, but that goal is subordinate to its nationalist or political agenda. Its leaders have differentiated the creation of an Islamic society from the goal of an Islamic state,[95] since they state it lacks the means to do so, and must ascertain the will of the people.

It appeals to various segments of Palestinian society which is also polyglot, riven by its division between those who remained in their original homes, or fled within Palestine, and refugees. The refugees outside of the West Bank and Syria comprise a very large number, have supported both the trends of armed conflict and negotiation, and live in varying circumstances. They are treated as citizens in Jordan, but not in Lebanon or Syria. HAMAS has refused to exclude them from the issue, as was essentially forced on other Palestinians attempting to negotiate with Israel. Within Gaza and West Bank, the camp issue and developmental needs of society mean greater public support for whatever political entity appears most effective, which has been HAMAS in recent years. As with Israelis, each sector of society—professionals, workers, camp refugees, students, members of the historic elites, and unemployed or underemployed youth—are divided in their views about their historical experience and future. Individuals' life-histories reveal that many of the young men involved in militance since the Second Intifadha are torn between what they see as the primacy of the conflict and normal desires for stability and their family needs.[96] Among youth, there is a distinct difference between Israelis who live with, it is true, an existential threat imparted through their society, and high school and military training, but who do not live, as Palestinian youth often do, in such a stressful state of emergency.[97] Stories of those Palestinians so traumatized that they cannot leave their apartments or homes are not limited only to HAMAS' members or their families. Palestinians' frequent imprisonment places a lot of stress on families.

One al-Aqsa commander I interviewed had been fighting since the age of 13. He was on the run, eluding PA security who had tortured and imprisoned his men, and he spoke to me of the brevity of his visits with his wife who, along with her family members, is hearing-impaired, and he would like to find software to help her.[98] In fact, HAMAS provided aid to numerous female family members during the chaotic and corrupt 2004-05 period, when women were harassed when they came to collect prisoners' stipends from PA officials.

One can point to diverse "hard-liners" who think that militaristic Israel can only understand force. Alongside them are professionals and others who have tried to use the new global connectivity—the media, internet, messaging—to their advantage, and believe in negotiation but who are worn down by the endless cycles of negotiating and dialoging that seem never to erode Israeli inflexibility and paranoia. For Palestinians, their Arab, Muslim, and Palestinian identities all carry negative weight and instant stereotyping in any interaction with Israel. The Arab and Palestinian parts of their identities were recovered and honored through political activism. HAMAS has allowed them to express their Muslim identity as well. Being outside the fractious pro- and anti-Arafatist struggle, the socialist-Arab, or Arab-nationalist versus others dynamic, and the conflict between Tunisian returnees versus Territory-based operatives of Fatah, also lent credence to HAMAS, whose leaders have earned their reputation for decency, practicality, and hard work in public service.

Recognition.

It is frequently stated that Israel or the United States cannot "meet" with HAMAS (although meeting is not illegal; materially aiding terrorism is, if proven) because the latter will not "recognize Israel." In contrast, the PLO has "recognized" Israel's right to exist and agreed in principle to bargain for significantly less land than the entire West Bank and Gaza Strip, and it is not clear that Israel has ever agreed to accept a Palestinian state. The recognition of Israel did not bring an end to violence, as wings of various factions of the PLO did fight Israelis, especially at the height of the Second (al-Aqsa) Intifadha.

Recognition of Israel by HAMAS, in the way that it is described in the Western media, cannot serve as a formula for peace. HAMAS moderates have, however, signaled that it implicitly recognizes Israel, and that even a *tahdiya* (calming, minor truce) or a *hudna*, a longer-term truce, obviously implies recognition.[99] Khalid Mish`al states, "We are realists," and there "is an entity called Israel," but "realism does not mean that you have to recognize the legitimacy of the occupation."[100]

The issue is fraught with tension for HAMAS. Tension came to the fore when observers interpreted HAMAS' participation and signing of the so-called Prisoner's Document (*National Conciliation Document of the Prisoners*) in 2006 (second version June 28, 2006),[101] which suggests just this implicit interpretation of recognition of Israel. Due to that popular perception, HAMAS removed its signature; however, the document has been the basis of various sets of negotiations, as in Qatari Shaykh Hamad's 2006 initiative.

Two States.

HAMAS has come to accept a two-state vision, even with the contradiction in terms between this aim and the rights of historic Palestine. Mish`al was asked,

> Do you accept a solution based on two states, an Israeli and a Palestinian, according to President George Bush's vision?
>
> [Mish'al] As a Palestinian, I am concerned with the establishment of a Palestinian state and not concerned with the occupation state. Why is the Palestinian being asked and the establishment of two states becomes one of his objectives and principles? The Zionist state exists. I am talking about my absent Palestinian state. I was the one deprived of my state, sovereignty, independence, freedom and self-determination. Therefore we ought to concentrate on how to achieve our rights. I am concerned with the establishment of my state.
>
> [Humaydi (interviewer)] Do you agree with Prime Minister Isma'il Haniyah's remarks: A Palestinian state within the 1967 territories and a truce?

> [Mish'al] This is a stand in the movement and it was adopted inside it. The movement accepts a state within the 1967 borders and a truce.[102]

Mistakes.

Excesses in attacks, particularly suicide attacks, on civilians are not acknowledged as crimes or tactical errors by HAMAS, but it is defensive when discussing this issue even when the "martyrs" are not HAMAS members. I have suggested in this monograph that HAMAS' use of violence, and potential relinquishing of violence, is best analyzed at the level of the group, or social movement, and not at the level of the individual. However, much of the literature on radicalization and deradicalization published since 9/11 provides analysis at the individual level. In the Palestinian case, some proffer the most negative insights on repression in Arab society which is supposed to produce violence, and that the glorification of the martyr is a part of ongoing Arab and Palestinian socialization. All of this may be true, but it does not deal with either the facts of occupation which result in direct harm, and human and material loss to Palestinians. Nor does this analysis help us understand the tactical use of violence, and how it can either decrease or increase.

Because they contradicted HAMAS' creed of Palestinian brotherhood, excesses in the fighting with Fatah and revenge activities, especially by lower level cadres in Gaza, were hard for HAMAS to live down, yet seemed to be fairly unavoidable, given the specific factionalization and identification of the strong Gaza clans.[103] Older securalists, various sectors of Arab Israelis, and those committed to any one of the other four parties of the PLO are not necessarily comfortable with HAMAS' dominance or vision, but can envision compromise, in which each respects the limitations of the other.[104]

HAMAS and Arab Political Currents.

The Ikhwan (Muslim Brotherhood) as a broader movement had garnered a great deal of support by championing the Palestinian cause, fighting in 1948 against Israel. But later, as the Ikhwan of Palestine turned towards missionary activity and away from armed resistance, it was the militant PLO that captured popular imagination and allegiances.

HAMAS turned the Ikhwan's survival equation on its head, asserting that the liberation of Palestine is an essential task for the *ummah,* or Muslim community, that rather than waiting for an Islamic society. Enacting the liberation of Palestine will bring about an Islamic way of life. Through this evolution, a certain amount of inter-Ikhwan and Ikhwan-HAMAS tensions emerged, especially in Jordan. These may take a new form, particularly if HAMAS begins negotiations with Israel which would possibly force a shift in the Brotherhood's position toward Israel, thus impacting Egypt and Jordan.

HAMAS' relations vis-à-vis the more secular nationalist movement also represents a dynamic forged over time. The PLO was eventually composed of three "progressive" groups, the Popular Front for the Liberation of Palestine (PFLP), the Democratic Front for the Liberation of Palestine (DFLP), and the Communist Party, along with the much larger organization, Fatah. Since all of Fatah's founders with the exception of Yasir Arafat had been members of the Ikhwan, Islamism was reflected in Fatah and appears in some of the discourse of the al-Aqsa Brigades which emerged from it.

Israel's decision to counter the results of the 2006 Palestinian election by boycotting HAMAS, withholding funds to the PA, and encouraging Mahmud Abbas to create his own nonelected government, have been described as a choice to support a "secular nationalist" movement as opposed to an Islamist nationalist movement which would not recognize Israel in the style demanded by that state. Supporting secularists versus Islamists is not the key to the issue. After all, Israel denied recognition of the PLO for years, likewise treating it as a terrorist movement.

The issue is the fundamentally altered relationship between the stronger Israel and the weak PA, given the PA's acceptance of negotiations and recognition of Israel through the Oslo process through which Israel thought it had solved its "internal Arab" dilemma. That change was threatened by both Intifadhas and then by HAMAS. HAMAS' transition from violence to political participation to a desire for negotiation really demonstrates a similar pattern, but HAMAS is holding back from formal recognition of Israel on the grounds that it must represent Palestinian popular will (or the will of its constituents).

Israel's interaction with HAMAS is an excellent example of the various lessons of asymmetric conflict that are highly instructive in the broader Middle East. The current situation is also a reflection of weaknesses or failings within Palestinian politics and society that include the aim of the PLO to serve as the sole representative of the Palestinian people, when, in fact, no party or government can ever maintain itself in such a hegemonic position indefinitely.

HAMAS' Troubles with Jordan.

HAMAS has had a mixed experience in Jordan which reflects the jockeying of Palestinian versus Jordanian interests and changes over time. In September 1997, four Israeli MOSSAD agents attempted to assassinate Khalid Mish`al, HAMAS' spokesman in Jordan, with electronically-delivered poison.[105] He was taken to the hospital, and when King Husayn was informed of the attack, he asked President Bill Clinton to force Israel to reveal the nature of the poison, and brought in a specialist from the Mayo Clinic. Husayn was infuriated by Israel's assumption that it could act freely in Jordan, despite (or possibly because of) the peace treaty, so he then called for the release of Ahmad Yasin.[106]

Since King Husayn's 1999 death, it is assumed that more American and Israeli pressure has been brought to bear on King Abdullah, his successor. The GID in Jordan waited for HAMAS officials to leave the country, as they knew the officials were to visit the Islamic Republic of Iran in 1999, and then raided and closed their offices and the offices of their publication and issued charges against them. Other leaders were forced underground. The Jordanian Ikhwan were divided as to the proper response, preferring not to have a break with the government.[107] This forced a transfer of HAMAS officials to Syria, including those who have taken more moderate positions on certain issues.

When Ibrahim Ghosheh left Qatar where he was in exile in 2001 and returned to Jordan, he was ordered to "freeze" his status in HAMAS and, if he did so, he could visit the Kingdom.[108] The Jordanians postponed an official visit by Mahmoud Zahar in April 2006 after the discovery of a weapons cache attributed to

HAMAS,[109] which included Iranian-made Katyushas. Whereas Mahmoud Abbas accepted the Jordanian claims, HAMAS rejected them and saw Jordan as playing into the Israeli-inspired dispute with Fatah. HAMAS' defense was that it has never been interested in fighting any battles (with other Arab entities) but only for Palestine.

HAMAS in Syria.

Syria has hosted Palestinian groups since 1967, and at times encouraged tensions with the mainstream of the PLO through its sponsorship of particular factions, its own Palestinian forces, and various forms of interference. Syrian and Palestinian actors in Syria were involved in the rebellion against Yasir Arafat, and the two factions conducted operations against each other though tensions have risen and waned. The Syrians were furious with Arafat when the Oslo Accords were announced. HAMAS, as well as Islamic Jihad, have offices in Damascus, publish there, and reportedly conduct training and planning there.

Khalid Mish`al (the unofficial leader of HAMAS today) and Musa Abu Marzuq (the deputy political leader) are located in Syria due to the practical need to maintain leadership "outside" of Palestinian territory and in light of changed circumstances in Jordan. Periodically U.S. statements appear indicating that Syria will have to rein in its support of "terrorist movements" to qualify for participation in peace negotiations with Israel—this message was conveyed by Speaker of the House Nancy Pelosi—or to be treated more cordially by the United States. Former U.S. President Jimmy Carter met with Marzuq, Mish`al, and Muhammad Nazzal for more than 4 hours in Damascus on April 18,

2008, and Carter urged that peace talks include both HAMAS and Syria.[110]

In June 2008, Syria's foreign minister, Walid Muellem, announced his country's support for the truce between HAMAS and Israel.[111] Despite the current excitement over a possible Israeli-Syrian détente and Syria's strong interest in recovering the Golan Heights, HAMAS officials were certain that the Syrian government would not abandon it, not even to clinch a peace deal, said Khalid Mish`al.[112] Bouthaina Shaaban, the Syrian Expatriate Minister, confirmed Syria's position that it will not abandon Hizbullah or HAMAS, and that such a demand in return for peace negotiations is like "asking the United States to shake off Israel."[113]

HAMAS and Saudi Arabia.

HAMAS receives a certain amount of support from Saudi Arabia. The United States has criticized the Kingdom for doing so, and in March 2006, a HAMAS delegation visited Riyadh where the Saudis made it clear that they attached no preconditions to support for the new government, and their aid to the poverty-stricken Palestinians is "humanitarian assistance."[114] Saudi funds were delivered to Palestinians by the Saudi Committee for the Support of the Al Quds Intifadha from 2000 to about 2006, thereafter by the Saudi Committee for the Relief of the Palestinian People, and will thereafter be under a monitored commission. The Committee partners with United Nations (UN) agencies such as the UN Educational, Scientific, and Cultural Organization (UNESCO) to provide scholarships, and the government recently promised funds to rebuild destroyed homes in Gaza and the West Bank.

HAMAS is likewise very concerned about its effective community and charitable efforts, and the attacks on these institutions in the West Bank[115] from August into September 2008 must concern Saudi Arabia.

Practicing Religion.

HAMAS' Islamist orientation is alive to the challenges Palestinians faced as Muslims. They lost control over their system of religious education and the appointment of clerics (which fell to Israel, Egypt, and Jordan). They could not visit numerous holy places, mosques, and tombs, many of which were closed. Palestinians in one area are blocked from travel to another, thereby preventing visits to religious sites or persons. They could not travel within the Arab world via Israel, and Palestinians who live in Israel are essentially cut off from the Arab world, except in very recent years when it is far easier for certain categories of Palestinians to travel to Jordan.

Palestinians have historically faced obstacles in performing the *hajj* (pilgrimage) to Mecca, one of the five basic requirements of Muslims. In 2002 Israel prevented all Palestinians under 35 from going on *hajj*. In November 2003, a large number of Palestinians (including women and elderly persons) were denied permission to go on the *'umrah* (the lesser pilgrimage) during Ramadan. In August 2007, 3,000 pilgrims were stranded at the crossing into Egypt. In late December 2007, over a thousand persons were not allowed entrance back into Gaza from Egypt. Egypt had allowed them into to its territory to perform *hajj*, but Israel had closed the border to punish HAMAS and, despite its promotion of Mahmoud Abbas, gave him no authority to solve the problem. This created a diplomatic headache for Egypt as Israeli Foreign Minister Tizpi Livni took Egyptians to task.[116]

Israel arrested certain Palestinian pilgrims, namely those thought to be HAMAS members, when reentering, which further illustrates their lack of sovereignty and Israel's willingness to embarrass Egypt and force it to pressure HAMAS by calling attention to the matters of the Gazan-Egyptian tunnels, Gilad Shalit, and other issues.

These problems—like the closure of mosques or blocking of Palestinian visitation to the Haram al-Sharif in Jerusalem in addition to summary detentions, individual and collective punishments, such as home-razings—fund the Muslim claim that Palestinians are being denied the rights to ordinary life and to practice their religion. This, Yusuf al-Qaradawi, the extremely popular Egyptian preacher watched avidly on Al-Jazeera, asserts is the reason that they may participate in individual or defensive *jihad,* which had been expressed through suicide attacks and other armed actions.

Political and Military Structure.

HAMAS is headed by a political bureau with representatives for military affairs, foreign affairs, finance, propaganda, and internal security. An Advisory Council, or Majlis al-Shura, is linked to the political bureau, which is also connected with all Palestinian communities, to HAMAS' social and charitable groups, HAMAS' elected members, district committees, and the leadership in Israeli prisons.

Major attacks against Israel have been carried out by the Izz al-Din al-Qassam Squads of HAMAS.

They also developed the Qassam rocket used to attack Israeli settlements and towns in the Negev desert. However, much of HAMAS' activity during the First Intifadha consisted of its participation within more broadly-based popular demonstrations and locally coordinated efforts at resistance, or countering Israeli raids, enforcing opening of businesses, and the like.

HAMAS protested the autonomy agreement between the Israelis and the PLO in Jericho and the Gaza Strip as too limited a gain. This put it into a more direct type of political confrontation with the PLO, and by the time of the first elections for the PA's Council in 1996, HAMAS was caught in a dilemma. It had gained popularity as a resistance organization, but the entire trajectory of PLO activities in Oslo 1 and Oslo 2 (the Taba Accord of September 28, 1995) were meant to end the Intifadha. The elections would further strengthen the PLO. However, if HAMAS boycotted the elections and most people voted, then it would be even more isolated. HAMAS' leadership rejected participation in those elections but without ruling it out in the future, and this gave the organization the ability to continue protesting Oslo and build up its political support. HAMAS presence in the universities, high schools, and professional groupings were important to it, and it even established women's organizations which rivaled and challenged the positions of Palestinian feminist groups in this era.[117]

When suicide attacks were launched to protest Israeli violence against Palestinians, HAMAS was blamed for inspiring or organizing the suicide bombers, whether or not its own operatives or those of the more radical Islamic Jihad were involved. In fact, HAMAS observed a 3-year moratorium on suicide attacks, which was then reestablished for a year, and possibly broken in a January 2008 attack in Dimona which may have been carried out by HAMAS or by other actors.

Suicide attacks are a terrorist tactic that multiplies the impact of a smaller force in an asymmetric struggle. They were first employed by the Tamil Tigers in Sri Lanka in the contemporary period, then in Syria against Syrian government targets, and in Lebanon against Israeli targets, and have spread in recent years to Iraq, Afghanistan, Jordan, Egypt, and Palestine although they were not a typical form of attack prior to this period, as suicide is not allowed in Islam. HAMAS operatives first utilized suicide attacks in 1994, after an American-born Israeli settler, Baruch Goldstein, fired on and threw hand grenades at unarmed worshippers in the al-Haram al-Ibrahimi mosque in Hebron on February 25, killing 29.[118] It was thought that Goldstein had attained entry with assistance of Israeli troops. Until that date, HAMAS' only targets were Israeli military. It ceased such attacks, which were very controversial with other Palestinians in 1995, and reintroduced them after the "targeted killing" of HAMAS leader Yahya Ayyash. Israeli sources aggrandized the themes of martyrdom to be found in Islamic history, and blamed much of contemporary Islamic radicalism and Palestinian psychology with its "culture of death."

HAMAS' leaders are defensive about the tactic, even though Palestinians appeared to support its use. The Norwegian group, Fafo, found that 69 percent of those Palestinians polled in 2005 agreed that attacks on Israeli targets where legitimate responses to the political situation. Thus it is clear that ordinary Palestinians see these attacks as being strategic, although they additionally expressed desperation.[119] HAMAS, like other Palestinian groups, argue that Israel has killed many more Palestinians than the other way around, and statistics show this to be true. From December 1987 to April 2006, Israel killed 5,050 Palestinians whereas Palestinians killed 1,426 Israelis.[120] It is clear that Israelis of lower economic means are more vulnerable to suicide attacks as these have frequently targeted buses.

Declarations of a *tahdiya* (calming) arranged by Alastair Crooke to end such attacks were made in 2002 and 2003. Crooke was the former Security Advisor to Javier Solana, the European Union High Representative. Crooke now heads Conflict Forum which advocates negotiating with HAMAS. Another *tahdiya* was held from March 2005, but the first two were broken when Israelis assassinated HAMAS leaders. Under the current truce, no attacks are being launched by HAMAS on Israel.

A *hudna*, or longer-term truce, (first offered by Shaykh Yasin) would be more encompassing and is conditional on cessation of attacks on civilians, a stop to settlement activities, and withdrawal from the Occupied Territories (the West Bank and Gaza).

Zakat and Community.

HAMAS' extensive array of social services are aimed at ameliorating the plight of the Palestinians. It provides funding for hospitals, schools, mosques, orphanages, food distribution, and aid to the families of Palestinian prisoners who, numbering more than 10,000 in these years, constituted an important political force. Given the PA's frequent inability to provide for such needs, HAMAS stepped into the breach.

Until its electoral triumph in January 2006, HAMAS received funding from a number of sources. Palestinians living abroad provided money, as did a number of private donors in the wealthy Arab oil states such as Saudi Arabia, Bahrain, and Kuwait, as well as those in the West. Much aid directed to renovation of the Palestinian territories was badly needed, but, unfortunately, a great deal of that rebuilding was destroyed in the Israeli campaign in the West Bank in 2002, which, in turn, was intended to combat the suicide bombings and the al-Agsa Intifadha.

Over the years the IDF has carried out "targeted eliminations" of a number of HAMAS leaders. These include Shaykh Yasin (March 22, 2004); Salah Shihada (July 23, 2002); Dr. Abd al-Aziz al-Rantisi (April 17, 2004); Dr. Ibrahim Al-Makadma (August 3, 2003); and Isma`il Abu Shanab (August 21, 2003). HAMAS has had to develop a capacity to replace leaders who were killed by Israel, and to recover damage to the organization. Beyond the previously mentioned HAMAS activities in Jordan and Syria, there also has been HAMAS activity in Palestinian refugee camps in Lebanon.

When United States cut off $420 million and the EU cut off $600 million in aid to the PA's HAMAS-led government, ordinary Palestinians experienced grave difficulties; food, medical supplies, gasoline, and energy were all impacted. Gaza had been impacted by poverty and high unemployment, with about 87.7 percent of all households living in income poverty by mid-2006, and about 61.5 percent said then that they lacked money for daily needs.[121]

To prevent total collapse, the United States and the EU promised relief funds, but these were hampered for a lengthy period. Gazans wrote about their difficulties; and the decision was made to risk blowing up in cabs running on cooking oil or simply to walk and to try to run aid activities without supplies or simply leave.

The latest attacks on charitable organizations in the West Bank must cease but that depends on an inter-Palestinian negotiation.

Hostages.

On March 12, 2007, the Army of Islam, a group with an al-Qa'ida-like orientation, under the protection of the Gazan Daghmush clan, kidnapped Scottish BBC correspondent Alan Johnston. They held him for 114 days, apparently thinking that Britain would agree to a trade for imprisoned leader Abu Qatada. HAMAS arranged Johnston's release after he was handed over to them in July.[122]

On July 25, 2006, IDF Corporal Gilad Shalit was captured by fighters who were variously announced as being from the Islamic Army, or fighters from that group, the Al-Aqsa Martyrs Brigade, and an umbrella group including HAMAS. HAMAS obtained custody of Shalit and could negotiate his release, but wanted concessions for doing so, namely a prisoner exchange and probably an opening to the Rafah border. Negotiations took place after the truce began, but stalled even though a prisoner exchange with Hizbullah was concluded. At the time of this writing, senior HAMAS official Ahmed Yousef had announced that there would be a prisoner exchange for Shalit by the end of Ramadan on October 1, 2008, possibly involving the return of HAMAS leaders from Syria to Gaza.

HAMAS' Threat Value.

Security analysts frequently exaggerate the threat of political organizations. What is the true threat of

HAMAS? Its forces were estimated in Gaza at only 5,000 to 6,000 fighters, which were just a fraction of the 168,000 of the IDF. In the summer of 2007, HAMAS vowed to double its numbers to 12,000. It may now be closer to 10,000 fighters, or other security analysts' figures of 15,000 fighters. In other words, we cannot accurately gauge its threat, except to say it is a much smaller force than the mighty IDF, even though its capacity goes beyond conventional fighting to small numbers who can engage in terrorist attacks. The Fatah Presidential Guard under Abbas numbered only about 3,700, and Abbas hoped to expand this by 1,000 with $86 million promised by the U.S. Government. That the Bush administration would provide $86 million to strengthen security forces loyal to Abbas, was reported in the world press.[123]

In March 2005, Shaul Mofaz accused HAMAS of obtaining *Strela* (SA-7) shoulder-fired anti-aircraft missiles.[124] Charges that HAMAS is gaining and stockpiling weapons in Gaza, including anti-aircraft missiles, are periodically reprinted in the Israeli press, with no ascertainable accuracy. However, the Qassam rockets that fell periodically on Sderot and surrounding Negev towns were real. Some American analysts also support the idea of an Israel reconquest of Gaza, with the justification that the group was building its strength and weapons capacity.[125] This argument makes sense only if one would also call for a new Israeli invasion of Lebanon, or for requiring an action by a UN force to disarm Hizbullah. None of these actions will lead to peace or security, and will not result in an end to HAMAS or Hizbullah.

The PA was authorized to have a police force and not an army. The dysfunctionality of that force stems from the PA's lack of sovereignty and the absence of a political solution with Israel, as much as technical deficiencies or problems of corruption.[126]

A future compromise will have to address Palestinian sovereignty. If Israel can never accept a Palestinian army but expects Palestinian self-policing to provide Israel security, one can only expect a large force that will be an employer to the many young men who have known nothing but armed resistance to Israel—as in, for example, the al-Aqsa Martyr's Brigades, which have operated under independent leadership varying by city or town.

HAMAS, the West, and the United States.

HAMAS shares an acceptance of the scientific rational traditions of the West along with moderate Islamist groups like the Muslim Brotherhood. (The fact that both groups are castigated as highly "fundamentalist" and Taliban-like is a great irritant to HAMAS.) HAMAS accepts the legitimacy of the nation-state, as opposed to bin Ladin and Zawahiri's emphasis on the Islamic nation. The Western training or Western-style education of most HAMAS leaders has much to do with the organization's stances.[127]

The United States had not initially labeled HAMAS a terrorist organization. The State Department acknowledged meetings with HAMAS representatives until March 1993[128] when Israelis protested. It was aware of Palestinians worldwide, who were either associated with the Ikhwan, or later, HAMAS. Palestinian organizations that were part of the PLO like the PFLP remained on the terrorist list, but practically speaking, the secular nationalist Palestinian groups were legitimated after Oslo despite certain factions' rejection of Oslo. HAMAS, which rejected Oslo but took a neutral stance toward the PA at the time, was increasingly treated as a dangerous terrorist threat in U.S. media from that point up to its victories in the 2006 and 2007 elections.

As a result of U.S. hostility to HAMAS, the organization increasingly regards the U.S. administration, although not the American people, as an enemy. However, HAMAS is not interested in a global jihad like al-Qa'ida, and maintains that its only foe is Israel, hoping that better communications with the United States will emerge, and recognizing that its officials' inability to travel and speak with Americans have damaged its image.[129]

The United States and Israel lobbied the EU to reject HAMAS. Under this pressure, the EU decided to reject the military wing of HAMAS, but not the organization as a whole; until 2003 and even later, certain European countries maintained ties with HAMAS.[130] Overall, the government-oriented or North Atlantic Treaty Organization (NATO)-oriented security analysts have taken a hard line toward HAMAS and seem slow to realize that backing President Abbas is a losing course.

Recommendations.

1. Let HAMAS fulfill its electoral promise to the Palestinians. The International Crisis Group recommended in the summer of 2006 that HAMAS be allowed to govern and should cease hostilities against Israel. Further, the boycott should end,[131] as it has caused terrible hardship for Palestinians.

2. The truce planned for 6 months and embarked on June 19, 2008, could be extended through diplomatic efforts. HAMAS wants Israel to cease military strikes and incursions into Gaza. Israel requires rocket and

mortar fire from Gaza into towns like Sderot to cease.[132] HAMAS needs to show evidence of substantial positive movement towards sovereignty, prisoner releases or other concrete benefits of the truce to its population, so U.S. policymakers and DoD should strongly support the use of this period for negotiations, as international obligations should not "be undertaken symbolically to rally support for an idea without furthering its attainment."[133]

3. HAMAS did not capture Corporal Gilad Shalit but acquired custody of him. (This should alert the international and the U.S. defense audience to the presence of far less controlled, and more extreme entities than HAMAS who might well create chaos in its absence.) While HAMAS held out in late September 2008 for a more significant prisoner exchange, it clearly aimed to redress the damage to its capabilities and the situation of a symbolically substantial number of prisoners. While some Americans have criticized the Israelis for negotiating for hostages, Yoram Schweitzer alludes to Israel's counter-aim of proving to its citizens that it will not fail in efforts to rescue them[134] given the military service needs of the state. Similarly, joint doctrine holds that diplomatic means, including negotiations, treaties or truces are possible ways to recover personnel.[135] HAMAS position is that the more than 11,000 Palestinian prisoners are, in essence, hostages. However, it must prevent its members and other groups from future hostage-taking. The increase in this tactic, like that of suicide attacks could forseeably continue. Hence U.S. policymakers or representatives acting in concert with Arab and European allies should do everything in their power to discourage the use of this tactic by Palestinians, and not only HAMAS, while convincing Israelis to release prisoners, particularly those of the political category.

4. Israel and the United States need to abandon their policies of non-negotiation and non-communication with HAMAS. A new American President should initiate a much more vigorous and dedicated program in which parties will agree to a sustained process which may take several years to complete, but which is decidedly preferable to the enormous social and economic cost of militaristic group politics that have burdened the Middle East for 6 decades.

5. U.S. policymakers and senior DoD leaders should heed certain lessons in the Palestinian-Israeli example as well as analytical failures of Israeli and Palestinian leadership. It is wrong to summarily replicate the Israeli strategy of seizing territories and enclaves and defending perimeters in other contexts, namely Iraq. Such "clear and hold" policies may appear to work in the short term, but will never produce the true security needed for nation-building. Just so Israel has asserted its authority over, and oppressed a people whose will to resist could not be quelled, no matter what military, counterterrorist, or collaborator-buying actions were pursued, as their effort lacked legitimacy.

Chaim Herzog characterized Israel as having a "civilian army" with inspired leadership in its first two wars (David Ben Gurion, Moshe Dayan), which "out-generaled" the Arabs, utilizing the indirect approach, improvisation and flexibility. He acknowledges the IDF's resulting overconfidence, and Egypt's brilliant use of deception in the 1973 War. But Herzog completely underestimates the Palestinian people in his summary of the insubstantial threat posed by the PLO in this same work, *The Arab-Israeli Wars*,[136] missing the very lesson that was oblivious to the French in Algeria, and which another Israeli leader, Ariel Sharon, vowed to get right. Characterizing popular resistance merely as terrorism, or the "long war,"[137] and facing it down with counterterrorist and barrier-based measures will not succeed in the long run. Locking up the Palestinians in their enclaves will only lead to another outburst of popular resistance, and has not protected the Israeli enclaves, just as no Green Zone, no *cordon sanitaire* can expect to be indefinitely secure.

6. Thus, the EU, the United States, Russia, and the UN should aid the conflicting parties in devising a new approach[138] to negotiations. This is important, for rather than standing shoulder-to-shoulder to the United States in postponing negotiations, the world's diplomatic practice needs ample revision, so that the third Intifadha and the seventh Arab-Israeli War need never be fought. The benefits of abandoning silence, boycotts, and secret coups would extend beyond the Arab-Israeli conflict to the issue of nuclear weapons and Iran and other rapprochements necessary to win the war on terror.

7. Moderates on both sides must be strengthened, but not under the selective and factionalizing methods recommended by the Quartet and Israel to date. Instead of just one specific final-solution oriented peace process, a whole variety of forums must be opened between Israelis and Palestinians, including HAMAS, with direct and indirect components that tap into the existing or past dialogue functions held in neutral locations so that, when negotiations are well underway, peacemaking, state-building, and economic plans will also be actualized.

8. The parties could consider an internationalization of Jerusalem with specific reference to the holy places there. The Palestinian and Israeli positions are far apart on the issue, but it is worth noting that in terms of international law, East Jerusalem was a part of the West Bank until its conquest and occupation in June

1967 under the Regulations of the Fourth Hague Convention of 1907, Articles 42 and 43; the Fourth Geneva Convention of 1949, Articles 1 and 2 (which Israel ratified in 1951); the First Protocol of 1977, Part 1; and UN Resolutions 2253 and 2254 and Security Council Resolution 252, which treats Israel's unification of Jerusalem as an illegal act.[139] This is the reason that other nations do not recognize Jerusalem as the capital of Israel and locate their embassies in Tel Aviv.

9. Jerusalem may be a more emotional issue than the matter of Palestinian refugees—except to the Palestinians, their refugees, and their descendents. HAMAS' position is that they must be considered and offered rights of return because those are the rights possessed by all Jews in the world today. HAMAS' officials have added, as do others, that it is very likely that not many would return, and that a staged process granting a set number per year could be established, thereby alleviating certain other long-standing situations in Lebanon and Syria, for example. A related solution is reparations for refugees, or both. These issues cannot be dealt with immediately, but should not be put off as in the Oslo process, or ignored or denigrated by Israelis to the extent that Palestinians lose trust in the other side.

10. Dismantling the settlements in the West Bank, and the corporate seizures and Israeli usage of land in the Jordan Valley which actually carves off a huge section of the West Bank, is essential to a resolution of the crisis.

11. The solution to the armed fighter presence in Palestinian society is to absorb HAMAS like other groups within the Palestinian security apparatus, but that rests on the acquisition of a national-unity government healing the HAMAS-Fatah rift as the

Saudi government had attempted in Mecca and a successful settlement as discussed. The dissolution of the al-Aqsa Brigades in the West Bank shows this can be done, even though there were serious rifts between Fatah-proper and the Brigades.

REFERENCES

Abdul Hadi, Mahdi. "Fateh and Hamas: A Coalition in the Making?" *Bitterlemons.org*, April 4, 2005.

Abdul Hadi, Mahdi, ed. *Documents on Jerusalem*. 4 Volumes. Jerusalem: PASSIA (Palestinian Academic Society for the Study of International Affairs), 2007.

Abu-Amr, Ziad. "Hamas: From Opposition to Rule." In Jamil Hilal, ed. *Where Now for Palestine? The Demise of the Two State Solution*. London: Zed Books, 2007.

_______. *Islamic Fundamentalism in the West Bank and Gaza Strip*. Bloomington: Indiana University Press, 1994.

_______. "Hamas: A Historical and Political Background." *Journal of Palestine Studies*, Vol. XXII, No. 4, Summer 1993, pp. 5-19.

Abu Sway, Mustafa. "Jerusalem: Crossroad of the World, An Islamic Perspective." A revised version of "The Holy Land, Jerusalem and Al-Aqsa Mosque in the Islamic Sources." *Journal of the Central Conference of American Rabbis*, Fall 2000, pp. 60-68.

Abu Toameh, Khalid. "Hamas: We Want Dialogue with US, EU." *Jerusalem Post*, December 10, 2007, *www6.lexisnexis.com/publisher/EndUser?Action=UserDisplayFullDocument&orgId=574&topicId=100023528&docId=l:714991365&start=12.*

Ahmad, Hisham. *Hamas*. Jerusalem: PASSIA, 1994.

Adel, Rania. "*Tirs croises de mesures.*" *Hebdo Al Ahram*. August 22-28, 2007.

Amayreh, Khaled. "PA Torments Palestinians on Israel's Behalf." Palestinian Information Center, July 31, 2008.

_______. "Inching Toward Implosion." *Al-Ahram Weekly*, December 28, 2006.

Amayreh, Khaled and, Dina Ezzat. "Chasing a Mirage?" *Al-Ahram Weekly*, July 10, 2008.

Alternative Information Center. "Interview with Palestinian Legislative Council Member, Hatem Qafisheh," July 26, 2007, *www.alternativenews.org/news/english/interview-with-palestinian-legislative-council-member-hatem-qafisheh-20070726.html*.

Associated Press. "Hamas Protesters in Gaza Warn Against Concessions to Israel." November 16, 2007.

Bar, Shmuel. *The Muslim Brotherhood in Jordan*. Tel Aviv: Moshe Dayan Center, Tel Aviv University, 1998.

Barghouti, Iyad. "Islamist Movements in Historical Palestine." In Abdel Salam Sidahmed and Anoushiravan Ehteshami, eds. *Islamic Fundamentalism*. Boulder, CO: Westview Press, 1996.

Barsky, Yehudit. "Hamas—The Islamic Resistance Movement of Palestine." American Jewish Committee, February 2006.

BBC. Hamas Burns Confiscated Drugs." BBC, December 9, 2007, *news.bbc.co.uk/2/hi/middle_east/7135431.stm*.

Beilin, Yossi. *The Path to Geneva: The Quest for a Permanent Agreement, 1996-2004*. New York: RDV Books, 2004.

Brecher, Michael. *The Foreign Policy System of Israel: Setting, Images, Process*. New Haven: Yale University Press, 1972.

Bishara, Azmi. "A Restructured PLO." *Al-Ahram Weekly*, June 21-27, 2007.

Blanchard, Christopher and Alfred Prados. "Saudi Arabia: Terrorist Financing Issues." *Congressional Research Service Report for Congress*, Updated September 14, 2007.

Brand, Laurie. *Palestinians in the Arab World: Institution Building and the Search for State*. New York: Columbia University Press, 1988.

Brom, Shlomo. "From Rejection to Acceptance: Israeli National Security Thinking and Palestinian Statehood." United States Institute of Peace, *Special Report* 177, February 2007.

_______. "A Hamas Government: Isolate or Engage? United States Institute of Peace. *USIPeace Briefing*, March 2006.

Brown, Nathan J. *Palestinian Politics After the Oslo Process: Resuming Arab Palestine*. Berkeley: University of California Press, 2003.

Brynen, Rex. *A Very Political Economy: Peacebuilding and Foreign Aid in the West Bank and Gaza.* U.S. Institute of Peace Press, 2000.

Bucaille, Laititia. *Growing Up Palestinian: Israeli Occupation and the Intifada Generation*. Princeton: Princeton University Press, 2006.

Chehab, Zaki. *Inside Hamas: The Untold Story of Militants, Martyrs and Spies*. London: I. B. Tauris, 1997.

Cohen, Amnon. *Political Parties in the West Bank under Jordanian Rule 1948-1967*. Ithaca, NY: Cornell University Press, 1980.

Collins, John. *Occupied by Memory: The Intifada and the Palestinian State of Emergency*. New York: New York University, 2004.

Cordesman, Anthony. "Palestinian Forces: PA and Militant Forces." Center for Strategic and International Studies (CSIS), February 1, 2006, pp. 6-11.

_________. *The Israeli-Palestinian War: Escalating to Nowhere*. Westport, CT: Praeger Security with CSIS, 2005.

Cramer, Richard Ben. *How Israel Lost. The Four Questions*. New York: Simon and Schuster, 2004.

Dicter, Avi and Daniel L. Byman. "Israel's Lessons for Fighting Terrorists and Their Implications for the United States." Brookings Institute, *Analysis Paper* 8, March 2006.

Dieterich, Renate. "The Weakness of the Ruled is the Strength of the Ruler: The Role of the Opposition in Contemporary Jordan." In George Joffé, ed., *Jordan in Transition*. New York: Palgrave, 2002.

El-Awaisi, Abd al-Fattah Muhammad. *The Muslim Brothers and the Palestine Question, 1928-1947*. London: I. B. Tauris, 1998.

Emerson, Steven. "Prepared Statement of Steven Emerson before the Senate Judiciary Committee Subcommittee on Terrorism, Technology and Government Information. Subject: Foreign Terrorists in America: Five Years after the World Trade Center Bombing." February 24, 1998.

Frisch, Hillel. "Motivation or Capabilities? Israeli Counterterrorism against Palestinian Suicide Bombings and Violence." *Mideast Security and Policy Studies*. Begin-Sadat Center for Strategic Studies, Bar Ilan University, December 2006.

______. "Has the Israeli-Palestinian Conflict Become Islamic? Fatah, Islam and the al-Aqsa Martyrs' Brigades." *Terrorism and Political Violence*, Vol. 17, No. 3, October 2005.

Gaess, Roger. "Interviews with Hamas." *Middle East Policy*, Vol. 9, No. 4, December 2002.

______. "Interview with Ismail Abu Shanab." *Middle East Policy*, Vol. 1, Issue 1, 1998.

Evens, Gareth and Robert Malley. "How to Curb the Tension in Gaza." *Financial Times*, July 6, 2006.

Franconia, Nick. "HAMAS's Military Capabilities after the Gaza Takeover." *PolicyWatch* #1278, Washington Institute of Near East Policy, August 27, 2007.

Ghanem, As`ad. "Israel and the Danger of Demography." In Gordon, Neve. "Ariel Sharon's Subjugation Strategy." *Baltimore Sun*, August 29, 2002.

_______. "No Negotiations." *In These Times*.

Gunning, Jeroen. *Hamas in Politics: Democracy, Religion, Violence.* London: Hurst and Co., 2007.

Hamad, Ghazi Ahmad. "The Challenge for Hamas—Establishing Transparency and Accountability." Geneva: Geneva Centre for the Democratic Control of Armed Forces, 2006.

al-Hamad, Jawad and Iyad al-Barghuthi, eds. *Dirasa fi al-fikr al-Siyasi li-Harakat al-Muqawama al-Islamiyya [HAMAS] 1987-1996.* (A Study of the Political Thought of the Islamic Resistance Movement [HAMAS] 1987-1996). Amman: Markaz Dirasat al-sharq al-awsat, 1997.

Al-Hamarneh, Ala. "The Social and Political Effects of Transformation Processes in Palestinian Refugee Camps in the Amman Metropolitan Area (1989-99)." In George Joffé, ed. *Jordan in Transition.* New York: Palgrave, 2002.

HAMAS. "*al-Haqiqa w-al-wujud.*" (The truth and the existence) 1990.

Hammer, Joshua. *A Season in Bethlehem: Unholy War in a Sacred Place.* New York: Free Press, 2003.

Hamzah, Dyala. "Is There an Arab Public Sphere?" In Armando Salvatore and Mark LeVine, eds., *Religion, Social Practice, and Contested Hegemonies: Reconstructing the Public Sphere in Muslim Majority Societies.* New York: Palgrave Macmillan, 2004.

Haniyeh, Isma'il. Letter to Raji Sourani of the Palestinian Centre for Human Rights (Gaza City). October 1, 2007, *www.pchrgaza.ps/files/PressR/English/2007/01-10-07.html.*

Hess, Amira. *Drinking the Sea at Gaza: Days and Nights in a Land Under Siege.* Elana Wesley and Maxine Kaufman-Lacusta, trans. New York: Henry Holt, 1999.

Herzog, Chaim. *The Arab-Israeli Wars: War and Peace in the Middle East from the War of Independence through Lebanon.* New York: Random House, 1982.

Herzog, Michael. "Can Hamas Be Tamed? *Foreign Affairs*. March/April, 2006.

Hilal, Jamil. "Hamas's Rise as Charted in the Polls, 1994-2005." *Journal of Palestine Studies*, Vol. XXXV, No. 3, Spring 2006.

Hilal, Jamil, ed. *Where Now for Palestine? The Demise of the Two State Solution*. London: Zed Books, 2007.

Hilal, Jamil and Mushraq Khan. "State Formation under the PNA." In Mushraq Khan, George Giacaman and Inge Ammundsen, eds. *State Formation in Palestine: Viability and Governance during a Social Transformation*. London: RoutledgeCurzon, 2004.

Hilal, Jamil, Saleh Al-Kafri, and Ellen Kuttab. *Unprotected Employment in the West Bank and Gaza Strip: A Gender Equality and Workers' Rights Perspective*. International Labor Organization, Regional Office for Arab States, Center for Arab Women Training and Research, June 2008.

Hochberg, Gil Z. *In Spite of Partition: Jews, Arabs, and the Limits of Separatist Imagination*. Princeton: Princeton University Press, 2007.

Hroub, Khaled. *Hamas: A Beginner's Guide*. London: Pluto Press, 2006.

________. "Hamas's Path to Reinvention." *OpenDemocracy*. September 10, 2006, *www.opendemocracy.net*.

_______. "A 'New Hamas' Through Its New Documents." *Journal of Palestine Studies*, Vol. XXXV, No. 4, Summer 2006.

_______. *Hamas: Political Thought and Practice*. Institute of Palestine Studies, 2000.

Hueston, Harry Raymond II, Paul G. Pierpaoli, Jr., and Sherifa Zuhur. "Hamas (Harakat al-Muqawama al-Islamiyya, Movement of Islamic Resistance)" in *Encylopedia of Arab-Israeli Wars*. Santa Barbara: ABC-Clio, 2008.

Hunter, F. Robert. *The Palestinian Uprising: A War by Other Means.* Berkeley: University of California Press, 1991.

Inbar, Efraim, ed. *Regional Security Regimes: Israel and Its Neighbors.* Albany: State University of New York Press, 1995.

Indyk, Martin. "Is Trusteeship for Palestine the Answer?" Brookings Institute.

International Crisis Group. "Inside Gaza: The Challenge of Clans and Families, *Middle East Report,* No. 71, December 20, 2007.

_______. "After Gaza." *Middle East Report,* No. 68, August 2, 2007.

_______. "After Mecca: Engaging Hamas." *Middle East Report,* No. 62, February 28, 2007.

_______. "Israel/Palestine/Lebanon: Climbing Out of the Abyss." *Middle East Report,* No. 57, July 25, 2006.

_______. "Palestinians, Israel, and the Quartet: Pulling Back from the Brink." *Middle East Report,* No. 54, June 13, 2006.

"Interview with Hamas Co-Founder Mahmoud Zahar: 'We Will Try to Form an Islamic Society'." *Spiegel Online International.* June 22, 2007. *http://www.spiegel.de/international/world/0,1518,490160,00.html*

"Interview with Mousa Abu Marzook." *Middle East Policy Journal,* Vol. 5, No. 2, 1997, p. 113.

Jad, Islah. "Between Religion and Secularism: Islamist Women of HAMAS." In Fereshteh Nouraie-Simone, ed. *On Shifting Ground: Muslim Women in the Global Era.* New York: Feminist Press, 2005.

Jamal, Amal. *Media Politics and Democracy in Palestine.* 2005.

______. *The Palestinian National Movement.* 2005.

Jamal, Manal. "Electoral Platforms, Ideologies, and Strategies: HAMAS and the 2006 Palestinian Legislative Elections." American Political Science Association, Chicago, August 31, 2007.

Jarbawi, Ali. "The Position of the Palestinian Islamists on the Palestine-Israel Accord. *Muslim World*, Vol. LXXXIV, Nos. 1-2, January-April, 1994.

Jensen, Michael I. "Islamism and Civil Society in the Gaza Strip," in Ahmad Moussalli, ed. *Islamic Fundamentalism: Myths & Realities*. Reading: Ithaca Press, 1998.

"Jerusalem 40 Years Later." *Palestine/Israel Journal of Politics, Economics and Culture*. Vol. 14, No. 1, 2007.

Karmi, Omar. "The Transformation of Hamas." *Wilberforce Quarterly*. Vol. 1, Issue 1, Summer 2006.

Kimmerling, Baruch. *The Invention and Decline of Israeliness: State, Society and the Military*. Berkeley: University of California Press, 2001.

Lake, Eli. "Hamas Takes Over Gaza Security Services." *New York Sun*, June 15, 2007, *www.nysun.com/article/56622*.

Legrain, Jean-François. "Hamas: Legitimate Heir of Palestinian Nationalism?" In John Esposito, ed. *Political Islam: Revolution, Radicalism, or Reform*. Boulder, CO: Lynne Rienner, 1997, pp. 159-178.

_______. "A Defining Moment: Palestinian Islamic Fundamentalism." In John Piscatori, ed. *Islamic Fundamentalisms and the Gulf Crisis*. Chicago: American Academy of Arts and Sciences, 1991.

Levitt, Matthew. *Hamas: Politics, Charity, and Terrorism in the Service of Jihad*. New Haven: Yale University Press, 2006.

_______. *Targeting Terror: U.S. Policy Toward Middle Eastern Sponsors and Terrorist Organizations Post-September 11*. Washington Institute for Near Eastern Policy, 2002.

Luft, Gal. "The Palestinian Security Services: Between Police and Army." *Middle East Review of International Affairs*, Vol. No. 3, June 2, 1999.

Lybarger, Loren D. *Identity and Religion in Palestine. The Struggle between Islamism and Secularism in the Occupied Territories.* Princeton: Princeton University Press, 2007.

Maddy-Weitzman, Bruce. "Slouching Towards Annapolis." Dayan Center of Tel Aviv University, *Notes*. October 30, 2007.

Mannes, Aaron. *Profiles in Terror: The Guide to Middle East Terrorist Organizations*. Lanham: Rowman & Littlefield, 2004.

Maoz, Zeev. "Evaluating Israel's Strategy of Low-Intensity Warfare, 1949-2006." *Security Studies*, Vol. 16, Issue 3, July 2007.

"Mecca Agreement." Jerusalem: Jerusalem Media and Communication Centre. February 8, 2007, *www.jmcc.org*.

Al Mezan Center for Human Rights. Field Work Unit. "Jungle of Guns & Law of the Jungle: Infringements upon the Law and the State of Insecurity in the Gaza Strip." Gaza, January 2007.

Mishal, Shaul. "The Pragmatic Dimension of the Palestinian HAMAS: A Network Perspective." *Armed Forces and Society*. Vol. 29, No. 4, Summer 2003, pp. 569-589.

Mishal, Shaul and Avraham Sela. *The Palestinian Hamas: Vision, Violence, and Coexistence*. New York: Columbia University Press, 2000.

Mitnick, Joshua. "Israel Weighs Tactics Toward Hamas." *Christian Science Monitor*, May 22, 2007.

________. "From Israeli Jails, Hamas Activists Press Middle Way." *Christian Science Monitor*, May 31, 2006.

________. "Islamic Jihad Steps Out From Hamas' Shadow." *Christian Science Monitor*, October 28, 2005.

Morris, Harvey. "Hamas Opts for Survival over Policy of Confrontation." *Financial Times*, July 27, 2007.

Muslih, Muhammad. *The Foreign Policy of Hamas*. New York: Council on Foreign Relations, 1999.

al-Naamy, Saleh. "Hamas versus Al-Qaeda." *Al-Ahram Weekly*, July 12-18, 2007, *weekly.ahram.org.eg/2007/853/re62.htm*.

Nafi, Basheer M. "Shaykh `Izz Al-Din Al-Qassam: A Reformist and a Rebel Leader." *Journal of Islamic Studies*, Vol. 8, No. 2, 1997.

Niva, Steve. "Surging Towards Gaza: How the U.S. is Reproducing Israel's Flawed Occupation Strategies in Iraq." *Foreign Policy in Focus*. April 23, 2008.

Nüsse, Andrea. *Muslim Palestine: The Ideology of Hamas*. Amsterdam: Harwood Academic Publishers, 1998.

Online Newshour. "Targeting Hamas." Margaret Warner, Meyrav Wurmser, Rashid Khalidi, and Glenn Robinson, July 23, 2002. *www.pbs.org/newshour/bb/middle_east/july-dec02/HAMAS_7-23.html*.

Parson, Nigel Craig. *The Politics of the PA: From Oslo to Al-Aqsa*. London: Routledge, 2005.

Paz, Reuven. "HAMAS's Lessons from Lebanon." *Policy Brief*. Peace Watch #262, Washington Institute for Near East Policy, May 25, 2000.

Pedahzur, Ami. *Suicide Terrorism*. Cambridge: Polity Press, 2005.

Peled, Alisa Rubin. *Debating Islam in the Jewish State: The Development of Policy Toward Islamic Institutions in Israel*. Albany: State University of New York Press, 2001.

Perry, Mark and Paul Woodward. "Document Details 'US' Plans to Sink HAMAS." *Asia Times*, May 20, 2007, available at *www.jerusalemites.org/articles/english/2007/May/20.htm*.

Polk,William. *A History of Insurgency, Terrorism and Guerilla War from the American Revolution to Iraq*. New York: Harper Collins, 2007.

Quigley, John. *Palestine and Israel: A Challenge to Justice*. Durham and London: Duke University Press, 1990.

Rand Palestinian State Study Team. *Building A Successful Palestinian State*. Santa Monica, CA: Rand Corporation, 2005.

Robinson, Glenn. *Building a Palestinian State: The Incomplete Revolution*. Bloomington: Indiana University Press, 1997.

________. "Humas as Social Movement," in Quintan Wiktorowicz, ed., *Islamic Activism: A Social Movement Theory Approach*. Bloomington: Indiana University Press, 2004.

Rose, David. "The Gaza Bombshell." *Vanity Fair*, April 2008, *www.vanityfair.com/politics/features/2008/04/gaza200804*.

Rosenfeld, Maya. *Confronting the Occupation*. 2004.

Roy, Sara. *The Gaza Strip: The Political Economy of De-Development*. 2001.

Said, Edward W. *The End of the Peace Process: Oslo and After*. New York: Vintage, 2001.

Salah, Mohammed, "Egypt, The PA, Hamas and the Hajj Pilgrims." *Al-Hayat*. January 1, 2008.

Sayigh, Yezid. *Armed Struggle and the Search for State: The Palestinian National Movement 1949-1993*. Oxford: Clarendon Press, 1997.

________."Inducing a Failed State in Palestine." *Survival*. 49:3 Autumn 2007.

Sha'ban, Ibrahim M. "Jerusalem in Public International Law." *Palestine-Isreal Jouranl of Politics, Economics and Culture,* Vol. 14, No. 1, 2007.

Shahak, Israel. *Open Secrets: Israeli Nuclear and Foreign Policies.* London: Pluto Press, 1997.

El-Shazly, Saad. *The Arab Military Option.* San Francisco: American Mideast Research, 1986.

Shipler, David. *Arab and Jew: Wounded Spirits in a Promised Land.* New York: Penguin, 2002.

Sucharov, Mira. "Security Ethics and the Modern Military: The Case of the Israel Defense Forces." *Armed Forces & Society,* Vol. 31, No. 169, Winter 2005.

Tamimi, Azzam. *HAMAS: A History from Within.* Northampton, MA: Olive Branch Press, 2007.

________. *Musharakat al-Islamiyyin fi al-sulta.* (The Islamists Participation in Power.) London: Liberty for the Muslim World, 1994.

Torstrick, Rebecca L. *The Limits of Coexistence: Identity Politics in Israel.* Ann Arbor: University of Michigan Press, 2000.

Tshirgi, Dan. *The American Search for Mideast Peace.* New York: Praeger, 1989.

Yiftachel, Oren. *Ethnocracy: Land and Identity Politics in Israel/ Palestine.* Philadelphia: University of Pensylvania Press, 2006.

Youngs, Richard. *Europe and the Middle East: In the Shadow of September 11.* Boulder, CO: Lynne Rienner, 2006.

Younis, Mona. *Liberation and Democratiation: The South African and Palestinian National Movements.* Minneapolis: University of Minnesota Press, 2000.

al-Zahar, Mahmoud. "No Peace Without Hamas." *Washington Post,* April 17, 2008.

Zuhur, Sherifa. "Hamas and the Two-State Solution: Villain, Victim or Missing Ingredient." With Shibley Telhami, Ali Abunimah, Haim Malka, and Charles Freeman (moderator). Vol. 15, No. 2, Spring 2008.

________. *Precision in the Global War on Terror: Inciting Muslims through the War of Ideas*. Carlisle, PA: Strategic Studies Institute, U.S. Army War College, 2007, *www.strategicstudiesinstitute.army.mil/pubs/display.cfm?pubID=843*.

________. *A Hundred Osamas: Islamist Threats and the Future of Counterinsurgency*. Carlisle, PA: Strategic Studies Institute, U.S. Army War College, 2006, *www.strategicstudiesinstitute.army.mil/pubs/display.cfm?pubID=636*.

________. "From Gaza to the West Bank: An Interview with Shaykh Hasan Youssef of HAMAS." *Strategic Studies Newsletter*, September 2005, reprinted in *Middle East Policy Council Journal*, *www.mepc.org*.

_________. "The Summit: Milestone or Mirage?" *Strategic Studies Newsletter*, October 2007.

_______. "Voices from Hamas." *Middle East Policy Council Journal* (Interview date, August 27, 2007), *www.mepc.org*.

ENDNOTES

1. Chaim Herzog, *The Arab-Israeli Wars: War and Peace in the Middle East: From the War of Independence through Lebanon*, New York: Random House, 1982, p. 362.

2. John Quigley, *Palestine and Israel: A Challenge to Justice*, Durham and London: Duke University Press, 1990, pp. 189-197.

3. I spent 11 months of this period in Israel/Palestine. So many aspects of the conflict appeared differently on the ground than as reported in Egypt or the U.S. However, I was especially struck by the predominant Israeli inertia towards peace, those who accepted the status quo and knew few, if any, "Arabs," and feared them. In contrast, I also encountered not insubstantial numbers of Israelis who opposed their government's positions and were working actively to make or maintain connections with Palestinians. See Zuhur, *An Outsider in Israel*, Institute of Middle Eastern, Islamic, and Diasporic Studies, in press.

4. B'tselem, The Israeli Center for Human Rights in the Occupied Territories, Statistics, *www.btselem.org*.

5. *Ibid*.

6. Whereas Palestinians suffered deaths and injuries in a far higher ratio than Israelis throughout the conflict, Israel was particularly concerned by deaths and injuries as a result of terrorist actions such as suicide bombings. In 2005 alone, there were 479 incidents, with 302 injuries and 74 fatalities, far more incidents than in Pakistan, Afghanistan, India, Thailand or Nepal for that year, however, with much lower incidences of death and injury. Source: *MIPT Terrorism Knowledge Base*, 2005.

7. Personal interview with Naser El-Din Shaer and Hatem Qafisheh, August 27, 2007, available at Middle East Policy website.

8. Khaled Amayreh, "PA Torments Palestinians on Israel's Behalf," Palestinian Information Center, July 31, 2008.

9. PCHR Weekly Report, July 31-August 6, *www.imemc.org/article/56429*.

10. Personal interview with Naser El-Din Shaer, August 11, 2008.

11. "PA Continues Its West Bank Arrest Campaign of HAMAS Supporters," *Report, PCHR,* August 11, 2008.

12. Gunning paints a parallel between HAMAS and Hegel in this insistence on structures. Jeroen Gunning, *HAMAS in Politics: Democracy, Religion, Violence*, London: Hurst and Co., 2007, pp. 88-89.

13. Khaled Hroub, *Hamas: Political Thought and Practice*, Washington, DC: Institute for Palestine Studies, pp. 26-33.

14. Glenn E. Robinson, "Hamas as Social Movement," in Quintan Wiktorowicz, ed., *Islamic Activism: A Social Movement Theory Approach*, Bloomington: Indiana University Press, 2004, pp. 126-127.

15. Shaul Mishal and Avraham Sela, *The Palestinian Hamas: Vision, Violence, and Coexistence*, New York: Columbia University Press, 2000, p. 157.

16. Islah Jad, "Mobilization without Sovereignty in the Oslo Period," in Sherifa Zuhur, *Women and Gender in the Islamic World*, Berkeley: UCIA and UC Press, 2003.

17. Dennis Ross, "Forward," in Matthew Levitt, *Hamas: Politics, Charity, and Terrorism in the Service of Jihad*, New Haven: Yale University Press, 2006, p. x.

18. Matthew Levitt, *Hamas: Politics, Charity, and Terrorism in the Service of Jihad*, New Haven: Yale University Press, 2006, p. 134.

19. Robinson, "Hamas as Social Movement," p. 128, citing Hroub, 2000, p. 241.

20. *New York Times*, October 21, 2007.

21. Robert J. Lieber, "The American Role in a Regional Security Regime," in Efraim Inbar, ed. *Regional Security Regimes: Israel and Its Neighbors*, Albany: State University of New York, 1995, p. 76.

22. Barry Rubin, "Israel's New Strategy," *Foreign Affairs*, Vol. 85, Issue 4, July/August 2006, pp. 111-112.

23. *Ibid.*

24. Statement by Israeli military personnel, June 2006.

25. William Polk, *Violent Politics: A History of Insurgency, Terrorism, and Guerilla War from the American Revolution to Iraq*, New York: HarperCollins, 2007; also see Uri Avnery, "An End Forseen," *Gush Shalom*, February 2, 2008.

26. It is useful to track the meetings between the U.S. Secretary of State and others and Abbas from fall 2006 onwards, along with commentary if one does not already accept the left/liberal or Arab media reports. For example, see *www.america.gov/st/texttrans-english/2006/October/20061004161011eaifas0.664303.html*.

27. Rushdi Abu Alouf and Richard Boudreaux, "Hamas Wins the Battle for Gaza Control," *Los Angeles Times*, June 15, 2007, p. A1.

28. International Crisis Group, "Inside Gaza: The Challenge of Clans and Families," Middle East Report No. 71, December 20, 2007.

29. BBC, June 18, 2008; *The Independent*, June 18, 2008.

30. Reuters, *Haaretz, New York Times*, August 13, 2008; *Global Research*, May 21, 2008, *www.globalresearch.ca/index.php?context=va&aid=9045*.

31. "Winograd Inquiry Commission Submits Interim Report," *Israeli Ministry of Foreign Affairs*, April 20, 2007, *www.mfa.gov.il/MFA/Government/Communiques/2007/Winograd+Inquiry+Commission+submits+Interim+Report+30-Apr-2007.htm*.

32. Israeli officials noted that the United States was interested in having it attack Syria in 2006, expanding the war on Lebanon, an idea some objected to. *Jerusalem Post*, July 30, 2006; *Christian Science Monitor*, August 9, 2006.

33. To the assertion that HAMAS continued rocket attacks on Israel: first, these were quieted, by and large, since June 2008, and even prior, many of these attacks are not launched by HAMAS but by Palestinian Islamic Jihad and other groups.

34. Meaning that it agrees with democratic freedoms so long as these are not "negative"—not harmful to the public order and morality. So its members follow *shari`ah* but are not imposing it on others. HAMAS is also controlling vigilante type actions in this regard. Gunning, pp. 84-88.

35. As in Nathan J. Brown, *Palestinian Politics After the Oslo Process: Resuming Arab Palestine*, Berkeley: University of California Press, 2003.

36. Sherifa Zuhur, "The Summit: Milestone or Mirage?" *Strategic Studies Institute Newsletter*, October 2007, *www.strategicstudiesinstitute.army.mil/pubs/display.cfm?pubID=824*.

37. Interviews, August 10-13, 2008; and see *Haaretz*, August 12, 2008.

38. As was promised by Shaykh Hasan Yousif prior to his incarceration. Personal interview, August 2005.

39. Rand Palestinian State Study Team, *Building A Successful Palestinian State*, Santa Monica, CA: Rand Corporation, 2005.

40. Haim Malka, "HAMAS and the Two State Solution," pp. 14, 18.

41. Anthony Cordesman, *Palestinian Forces: PA and Militant Forces*, Washington, DC: Center for Strategic and International Studies, p. 15.

42. Hroub, *Hamas*, p. 25.

43. Azzam Tamimi, *Hamas: A History from Within*, Northampton, MA: Olive Branch Press, 2007, pp. 45, 49.

44. Ibrahim al-Maqadmeh, who had revealed Yasin under torture, was sentenced to 8 years in jail.

45. Whereby 1,150 Palestinian prisoners were released in exchange for 3 Israelis held by the Palestinian Front for the Liberation of Palestine-General Command. The exchange was considered to be an initiative of Shaykh Yasin.

46. Hroub, *Hamas*, p. 36.

47. Basheer M. Nafi, "Shaykh `Izz Al-Din Al-Qassam: A Reformist and a Rebel Leader" *Journal of Islamic Studies*, Vol. 8, No. 2, 1997, pp. 185-215.

48. Jihad by the sword is terminology for Western consumption, but makes clear that the jihad of individual striving to be a good Muslim is also commanded, and distinct. See John Kelsay, *Arguing the Just War in Islam*, Cambridge, MA: Harvard University Press, 2007.

49. "The Movement of Islamic Jihad and the Oslo Process: An Interview with Ramadan Abdullah Shallah, *Journal of Palestine Studies*, Vol. 28, 1999, pp. 61-73. Ziad Abu-Amr, *Islamic Fundamentalisms in the West Bank and Gaza: Muslim Brotherhood and Islamic Jihad*, Bloomington: Indiana University Press, 1994.

50. Tamimi, p. 36.

51. Mishal and Sela, *The Palestinian Hamas*, p. 21.

52. Tamimi, p. 38.

53. Amira Hass, *Drinking the Sea at Gaza: Days and Nights in a Land Under Siege*, Elana Wesley and Maxine Kaufman-Lacusta, trans., New York: Henry Holt, 1999, p. 217.

54. *Ibid*, pp. 208-217.

55. Sela and Mishal, p. 26.

56. Tamimi, p. 30.

57. *Ibid*, p. 33.

58. Khalid Hroub explains that the HAMAS leaders never utilize the phrase, "the destruction of Israel," although HAMAS' outdated charter (which they also refrain from citing) suggests such an intent. Khaled Hroub, *Hamas: A Beginner's Guide*, London: Pluto Press, 2006, p. 38.

59. Andrea Nüsse, *Muslim Palestine: The Ideology of Hamas*, Amsterdam: Harwood Academic Publishers, 1998.

60. *Ibid.*, pp. 49-52.

61. Nels Johnson, *Islam and the Politics of Meaning in Palestinian Nationalism*, London: 1982, p. 31.

62. *Falastin Muslima*, June 1990, p. 11; *Ibid.*, July 1990, p. 29; *Ibid.*, August 1990, pp. 45. At that time, only some 200,000 immigrants had arrived, but their increasing numbers have altered Israel's demography and swung politics further to the right.

63. *Ibid.*, January 1990.

64. Khalid Mish'al in interview with Azzam Tamimi, Damascus, August 14, 2003; see Tamimi, p. 149.

65. Ibrahim Ghosheh in interview with Azzam Tamimi, Amman, August 21, 2003; see Tamimi, p. 149.

66. Tamimi, pp. 265-270.

67. *Ibid.*, pp. 271-283.

68. *Ibid.* pp. 271-279.

69. *Ibid.*, p. 280.

70. *Falastin al-Muslima*, March 1990, p. 10.

71. Nikki Keddie, " Autobiographical Interview," in *Women in the Middle East: Past and Present*, Princeton: Princeton University Press, 2007, p. 343.

72. Nüsse, p. 106; also see Ellen McLarney, "Women's Emancipation in Islamic Writings," presented at the Middle East Studies Association meetings, Montreal, Canada, November 19, 2007.

73. Hroub, p. 74.

74. Nüsse, pp. 101-104.

75. Interview with Shaykh Hasan Yousif, Ramallah, August 2005.

76. Despite the title, the following article is a pretty good description of fears and realities at the outset of 2006. Lauren Gelfond Feldinger, "Days of Hamas: Christians under Cover," *Newswire*, February 27, 2006, *www.natashatynes.com/newswire/2006/02/days_of_HAMAS_c.html*.

77. Hroub, *Hamas for Beginners*, p. 73.

78. *Ibid.*, p. 78.

79. Islah Jad, "Between Religion and Secularism: Islamist Women of Hamas," Fereshteh Nouraie-Simone, ed., *On Shifting Ground: Muslim Women in the Global Era*, New York: Feminist Press, 2005.

80. Zaki Chehab, *Inside Hamas: The Untold Story of Militants, Martyrs, and Spies*, London: I. B. Tauris, 1997, p. 115.

81. *Ibid.*, pp. 96-97.

82. Interview of Khalid Mishal by Ibrahim Muhaydi in Damascus on October 10, 2006, published in *al-Hayut*, October 12, 2006.

83. David Rose, "The Gaza Bombshell," *Vanity Fair*, April 2008, *www.vanityfair.com/politics/features/2008/04/gaza200804*.

84. *Al-Majd*, "Action Plan for the Palestinian Presidency," April 30, 2007; see also Mark Perry and Paul Woodward, "Document Details 'US' Plans to Sink HAMAS," *Asia Times*, May 20, 2007.

85. Sarah El Deeb, *Associated Press*, June 14, 2007.

86. Ziad Abu-Amr, "Hamas: From Opposition to Rule," in Jamil Hilal, ed., *Where Now for Palestine? The Demise of the Two State Solution*, London: Zed Books, 2007.

87. Larry Derfner, "The Assassination of Sheikh Yassin: Sharon Opens the 'Gates of Hell'; Fear and Loathing in Israel," *Washington Report on Middle East Affairs*, Vol. 23, No. 4, 2004, pp. 12-15.

88. Robinson, *Building a Palestinian State*, p. 193.

89. Baruch Kimmerling, *The Invention and Decline of Israeliness: State, Society, and the Military*, Berkeley: University of California Press, p. 2.

90. *Ibid.*, Chapters Six and Seven, pp. 173-228.

91. Steve Niva, "The 'Israelization' of U.S. Military Doctrine and Tactics: How the U.S. is Reproducing Israel's Flawed Occupation Strategies in Iraq," *Foreign Policy in Focus*, April 21, 2008.

92. See Mira Sucharov, "Security Ethics and the Modern Military: The Case of the Israeli Defense Forces." *Armed Forces & Society*, Vol. 31, No. 169, Autumn 2005.

93. *Ibid.*

94. HAMAS Political Bureau, "The Islamic Resistance Movement (HAMAS)," 2000.

95. "Interview with HAMAS Co-Founder Mahmoud Zahar: 'We Will Try to Form an Islamic Society'," *Spiegel Online International*, June 22, 2007, *www.spiegel.de/international/world/0,1518,490160,00.html*.

96. Laititia Bucaille, *Growing Up Palestinian: Israeli Occupation and the Intifada Generation*, Princeton: Princeton University Press, 2006.

97. John Collins, *Occupied by Memory: The Intifada and the Palestinian State of Emergency*, New York: New York University, 2004.

98. Personal interview, Ramallah, July 2005.

99. Personal interviews, 2005-07.

100. Khalid Mish'al interviewed by Ibrahim Humaydi, Damascus, October 10, 2006, published in *al-Hayat*, October 12, 2006.

101. "Full Text of the National Conciliation Document of the Prisoners, June 28, 2006," Jerusalem Media and Communication Centre, *www.jmc.org/documents/prisoners2.htm*.

102. *Al-Hayat*, October 12, 2006.

103. International Crisis Group, "Inside Gaza: The Challenge of Clans and Families," *Middle East Report*, No. 71, December 20, 2007.

104. Distillation of comments in interviews carried out in 2007-08.

105. *New York Times*, February 25, 1998 (when the Mossad chief, Danny Yatom resigned); "Profile: Khaled Meshaal of HAMAS," *BBC*, February 8, 2006, *news.bbc.co.uk/1/hi/world/middle_east/3563635.stm*; Tamimi, *HAMAS*, pp. 104-111.

106. Tamimi, *Hamas*, pp. 104-111; P. R. Kumaraswamy, "Tension Returns Between Jordan and Hamas," *Power and Interest News Report*, July 13, 2006.

107. Tamimi, *Hamas*, p. 127.

108. P. R. Kumaraswamy, "The Jordan-Hamas Divorce," *Middle East Intelligence Bulletin*, Vol. 3, No. 8, August/September 2001.

109. *International Herald Tribune*, April 20, 2006; Kumaraswamy, "Tension Returns."

110. *AFP*, April 19, 2008.

111. *Middle East Times*, June 20, 2008.

112. *Reuters*, June 18, 2008.

113. *Jerusalem Post*, June 17, 2008.

114. *BBC*, and *Turkish Daily*, March 11, 2006; Christopher Blanchard and Alfred Prados, "Saudi Arabia: Terrorist Financing Issues," *CRS Report for Congress*, September 14, 2007, pp. 9-12.

115. Personal interviews and observations, August 2008.

116. Mohammad Salah, "Egypt, The Palestinian Authority, HAMAS And The Hajj Pilgrims," *al-Hayat*, February 1, 2008.

117. Islah Jad, "Between Religion and Secularism: Islamist Women of Hamas," Fereshteh Nouraie-Simone, ed., *On Shifting Ground: Muslim Women in the Global Era*, New York: Feminist Press, 2005.

118. Hroub, *Hamas: A Beginner's Guide*, p. 52.

119. Tamimi, pp. 161-163; see also Gro Hussel Knippe, "Palestinian Opinions on Peace and Conflict, Internal Affairs and Parliament Elections 2006. Results from Fafo polls in September and November-December 2005" Fafo, 2006, p. 2.

120. Of the dead, 137 were Israeli children and 998 were Palestinian children. *Ibid*, p. 55, based on figures from B'tselem, an Israeli human rights organization.

121. Jamil Hilal, Saleh al Kafri, and Eileen Kuttab, *Unprotected Employment in the West Bank and Gaza Strip: A Gender Equality and Workers' Rights Perspective,* Strip, International Labour Organization Regional Office for Arab States, Center for Arab Women Training and Research, June 2008, p. 33.

122. BBC, July 7, 2007, *news.bbc.co.uk/2/hi/uk_news/6280222.stm.*

123. Wafa Amir, "Abbas Declares Hamas Force Illegal," *Reuters,* July 7, 2007.

124 . Steven Erlanger, "Israeli Says Palestinians Smuggle Antiaircraft Missiles Into Gaza," *New York Times,* March 29, 2005.

125. Nick Franconia, "Hamas's Military Capabilities after the Gaza Takeover," *PolicyWatch* #1278, Washington Institute of Near East Policy, August 27, 2007.

126. For the background of the Palestinian Security Forces in the West Bank and Gaza, see Brynjar Lia, *A Police Force Without a State,* Reading: Ithaca Press, 2006.

127. Hroub, *Hamas,* pp. 108-110.

128. *Boston Globe,* March 3, 1993.

129. Hroub, *Hamas,* p. 112; author's personal interview with Hasan Yousef, August 2005; author's personal interviews with Naser el-Din al-Shaer and Hatem Rabah Qafishah, August 2007.

130. Hroub, *Hamas,* p. 113.

131. Gareth Evens and Robert Malley, "How to Curb the Tension in Gaza," *Financial Times,* July 6, 2006. Similar views to those expressed by William Arkin, August 7, 2006, *blog.washingtonpost.com/earlywarning/2006/08/let_hezbollah_and_HAMAS_govern.html,* were found throughout the Middle Eastern press.

132 . *New York Times,* June 18, 2008.

133. *National Security Strategy*, 2002; and Multinational Operations, Additional Doctrine, JP 3-16, Chapter 1, Paragraph 1.

134. In reference to the Hizbullah-Israeli exchange, Yoram Schweitzer, "Not That Bad a Deal," *Jerusalem Post*, July 23, 2008.

135. U.S. Department of Defense *Joint Publication 3-50*, p. 1-3.

136. Herzog, *The Arab-Israeli Wars*, pp. 362-368.

137. As in the *Quadrennial Defense Review* of 2006. Other than the targeting of terrorist networks, we see here only the recommendation outside Iraq and Afghanistan of the same "indirect approach" mentioned by Herzog, with the example of Allenby's attack on Aqaba. Granted, the term "long war" was relinquished within U.S. Central Command, but persists as a concept elsewhere.

138. As the International Crisis Group had earlier urged as well, "Israel/Palestine/Lebanon: Climbing Out of the Abyss," *Middle East Report* No. 57, July 25, 2006.

139. Ibrahim M. Sha`ban, "Jerusalem in Public International Law," *Palestine-Israel Journal of Politics, Economics and Culture*, Vol. 14, No. 1, 2007, pp. 43-44.